A History of Silence

D1570205

A History of Silence

From the Renaissance to the
Present Day

Alain Corbin

Translated by Jean Birrell

polity

First published in French as *Histoire du silence. De la Renaissance à nos jours* © Éditions Albin Michel, Paris, 2016

This English edition © Polity Press, 2018

Polity Press
65 Bridge Street
Cambridge CB2 1UR, UK

Polity Press
101 Station Landing
Suite 300
Medford, MA 02155, USA

ISBN-13: 978-1-5095-1735-0
ISBN-13: 978-1-5095-1736-7 (pb)

A catalogue record for this book is available from the British Library.

Typeset in 11 on 14 pt Sabon by
Servis Filmsetting Ltd, Stockport, Cheshire
Printed and bound in ????????????????

The publisher has used its best endeavours to ensure that the URLs for external websites referred to in this book are correct and active at the time of going to press. However, the publisher has no responsibility for the websites and can make no guarantee that a site will remain live or that the content is or will remain appropriate.

Every effort has been made to trace all copyright holders, but if any have been inadvertently overlooked the publisher will be pleased to include any necessary credits in any subsequent reprint or edition.

For further information on Polity, visit our website: politybooks.com

Contents

In silence there is always something unexpected, a beauty that catches you unawares, a tonality to be savoured with the finesse of a gourmet, an exquisite repose . . . never automatic, it happens as if impelled by some inner force. Silence descends . . . it comes softly and silkily.

Jean-Michel Delacomptée
Petit éloge des amoureux du silence

Acknowledgements

I would like to thank Fabrice d'Almeida for his careful editing of the final version of this book and Sylvie le Dantec for her help with the preparation of the manuscript.

Prelude

Silence is not simply the absence of noise. We have almost forgotten what it is. Sound cues have changed their nature, become weaker and lost religious significance. The fear, even dread, caused by silence has intensified.

In the past, the people of the West savoured the depth and the qualities of silence. They saw it as the precondition for contemplation, for introspection, for meditation, for prayer, for reverie and for creation; above all, they saw it as that inner space from which speech came. They scrutinized its social tactics. For them, painting was silent speech.

The intimacy of places, that of the bedroom and its furniture, like that of the house, was bound up with silence. With the rise of the sensitive soul in the eighteenth century, and inspired by the cult of the sublime, people began to appreciate the many different silences of the desert and to listen to those of the mountains, the sea and the countryside.

Silence testified to the intensity of a love affair and

seemed a precondition for fusion. It foretold the lasting nature of the emotion. The life of the invalid, the proximity of death and the presence of the tomb gave rise to a range of silences, which survive today only in vestigial form.

What better way could there be to experience them than to immerse ourselves in quotations from some of the many authors who have embarked on a veritable aesthetic quest? Reading them, we put our own sensibility to the test. History has too often claimed to explain. When it tackles the world of the emotions, it must also and primarily make people feel, especially when the mental worlds have disappeared. This makes a large number of revealing quotations indispensable. They alone can enable the reader to understand how people experienced silence in the past.

It is difficult to be silent today, which prevents us from listening to the inner speech that calms and soothes. Society enjoins us to accept noise in order to be part of the whole, rather than to listen to ourselves. Thus the very structure of the individual is modified.

True, a few solitary walkers, artists and writers, practitioners of meditation, those who have withdrawn to a monastery, a few women who visit graves and, above all, lovers who gaze wordlessly at each other are in search of silence and remain sensitive to its qualities. But they are like travellers washed up on what will soon be a desert island, whose shores are wearing away.

The main culprit is not, however, as might be thought, an intensification of the general noisiness of urban life. Thanks to activists, legislators, hygienists and decibel-measuring technicians, city noise is now different but probably no more deafening than in the nineteenth century. What is new is hyper-mediatization and permanent connectivity and, in consequence, the incessant flow of words that is thrust on people and which makes them dread silence.

My evocation in this book of the silence of the past and of how people searched for it, and of the qualities, disciplines, tactics, richness and power of the speech of silence, may help us to relearn how to be silent, that is, to be ourselves.

1

Silence and the Intimacy of Places

There are specific places where silence makes its subtle omnipresence felt, where it can be more easily heard, where it may appear as a sweet, soft, continuous and anonymous sound; places to which the advice of the poet Valéry applies: 'Listen to this delicate sound which is continuous, and which is silence. Listen to what you hear when nothing makes itself heard'; this noise 'blankets everything, this sand of silence ... Now nothing. This nothing is huge in the ears.'[1] Silence is a presence in the air. It is 'not visible', wrote Max Picard, 'and yet its existence is clearly apparent. It extends to the furthest distances, yet is so close to us that we can feel it as concretely as we feel our own bodies.'[2] It is not only thought and ideas that are affected; behaviour and decisions are also subject to its strong influence.

Among the places where silence particularly makes itself felt are the house, with its rooms, hallways and bedrooms, and all the objects that furnish it, but also certain specific buildings, such as churches, libraries, castles and prisons. I shall begin by quoting examples

---

of what was said of these places in the nineteenth and twentieth centuries, a time when discussion of the silence of intimate places intensified. I will reserve for later the silence that is associated with contemplation and interiority, and is a precondition for meditation, prayer and listening to the word of God.

There are houses that breathe silence, where it seems to permeate the walls. This has been powerfully conveyed in our own day by the paintings of Edward Hopper. It is equally the case with Quesnay, the house of the married priest described by Barbey d'Aurevilly: it was 'in the silence of this house where silence had always held such sway' that the hero, Néel de Néhou, awaiting the return of Sombreval, watched over Calixte.[3]

Silence was central to the work of Georges Rodenbach, for example that of the patrician residences of Bruges. All along the canals, in this dying town, the silence of these hushed houses oppresses; walking the deserted streets, the novel's main character, Hugues Viane, 'found himself the brother in silence and in melancholy of this doleful Bruges'.[4] Here, says Rodenbach, silence is something living, real, despotic, hostile to anything that disturbs it. In this town, every sound shocks, is sacrilegious, crude and gross.

The presence of silence is crucial to Julien Gracq's novel *The Opposing Shore*.[5] It reigns in the palace, Vanessa's old home, all over the town of Maremma in which it stands and in the capital, Orsenna, in fact everywhere where the decadence can be felt. I will return to this novel, which is obsessed by many different forms of silence.

Inside houses, various types of silence impregnate rooms, halls, bedrooms and studies. The silence that is the main subject of the best-known novel of Vercors, *The Silence of the Sea*, lay heavy in the ground floor room in which the uncle and his niece awaited the German officer Werner von Ebrennac.[6] From the beginning, the German sensed it and he seemed 'to be gauging the depth of the silence' even before he entered the room. After he had spoken, the silence persisted; it 'was unbroken, it grew closer and closer like the morning mist; it was thick and motionless'; the immobility of the niece and the uncle 'made it even heavier, turned it to lead'.[7]

Silence then accompanies events as they unfold; it was the silence of France which the German officer struggled to overcome during 'more than a hundred winter evenings'. To this end, he accepted the implacable silence: 'let [it] invade the whole room, and, like a heavy unbreathable gas, saturate every corner of it'. It was as if, of the three protagonists, it was he who felt most at ease.[8] On his return, years later, having lived through various traumas and understood the resistance put up by France, Werner von Ebrennac now approves the 'healthy obstinacy' of the silence that 'once more fell', but which was now 'much more tense and thick'.[9] What had been, in 1941, the silence of dignity had become the silence of resistance.

'Every bedroom', wrote Claudel, 'is a huge secret.'[10] Indeed, bedrooms are the private space of silence par excellence. It is necessary to them. The nineteenth century, observes Michelle Perrot, saw the rise of the desire for a private bedroom, for personal space, a shell, a place of secrecy and silence.[11] This desire is historical fact. Baudelaire proclaimed the delight he felt when at last, in the evening, he was alone in the haven of his bedroom. There, he wrote, citing La Bruyère, he escaped 'the great woe of not being able to be alone', by contrast with those who lose themselves in the crowd, 'probably afraid they couldn't tolerate themselves'. 'Finally alone! Now only the rattling of some lingering and exhausted carriages can still be heard. For a few hours, we will possess silence, if not rest. Finally! The tyranny of the human face has disappeared, and now only I myself will make me suffer.' Then, 'annoyed with everyone and annoyed with myself, I long to redeem myself and to bolster my pride a bit in the silence and solitude of the night.'[12]

Huysmans attributes a similar desire to several characters in his novels. Des Esseintes surrounds himself with almost mute servants, old people weighed down by years of silence. He contrives a silent bedroom for himself: a rug, a padded ceiling and well-oiled doors ensure that he never hears the footsteps of the servants. He dreamed of 'a sort of oratory', a false 'monastic cell', a place of 'retreat for thoughts', though eventually he found the silence burdensome.[13]

Marcel Proust had the walls of his bedroom covered with cork and bribed the workmen not to do the jobs for which they were hired in the apartment above his. Kafka expressed the desire to have a hotel room that would allow him 'to isolate himself, say nothing, delight in silence and write at night'.[14]

Other writers have analysed in more detail the roots of this widespread desire for silence in a room of one's own. Its importance is often linked to the emotions stirred by the faint and familiar sounds emanating from members of the family. Walt Whitman acclaims 'the mother at home, quietly placing the dishes on the supper-table'.[15] Rilke describes the happiness he felt in the 'silent room of an ancestral house among the quiet things in their abiding places', hearing 'the tits sounding their first notes outside in the green and sun-shot garden, and away in the distance the village clock'.[16] Here, happiness comes from the osmosis between private space and an indeterminate external space.

Rilke also described the various silences created for a child by the mother's visit:

> O the silence on the staircase, the silence in the next room, the silence high up under the ceiling. O Mother: O you, the only one who dealt with all that silence, back in my childhood; who took it upon herself, saying: Do not be afraid – it's me; who had the courage, in the dead of night, to *be* that silence for one who was frightened, who was scared stiff. You light a lamp, and that sound is already you.[17]

There is, he said, another particular silence within a bedroom, the silence created when the neighbours stop making a racket: 'And now . . . silence fell. It was as silent as in the aftermath of pain. The silence was strangely palpable and prickling, as if a wound were healing.' It was a silence that came as a surprise and kept him awake; 'the nature of that silence had to be experienced; it cannot be described.'[18]

The narrator of *In Search of Lost Time* frequently analyses the nature of the silence that surrounds him. He savours the 'charming quality' of silence on the Legrandin terrace. In a much-quoted passage, he describes the interior of Tante Léonie's bedroom:

> The air of [this room] was saturated with the fine bouquet of a silence so nourishing, so succulent that I could not

enter . . . without a sort of greedy enjoyment, particularly
on those first mornings, chilly still, of the Easter holidays,
when I could taste it more fully, because I had just arrived
then at Combray.[19]

We shall return to the care with which the narrator
maintains his silence in the room in which Albertine
sleeps.

I shall also return to the subtle eroticism pervad-
ing the bedroom evoked by Barbey d'Aurevilly in
'The Crimson Curtain'. Here, I shall consider only the
various menacing silences inside the house, which is a
veritable kingdom of silences. The lover, awaiting the
silent arrival of Alberte, checks the 'terrifying silence' of
the sleeping house. He listens to the ominous silence of
the parental bedroom. Stealth was essential to avoid any
surprises, to prevent any noise from the creaking hinges
of the doors. Alberte's first appearance in the narrator's
bedroom comes when he is cocooned in the silence of
the room. The street itself was as quiet as 'the bottom of
a well'. 'I would have heard a fly move', he says, 'but if,
by chance, there happened to be one in my bedroom, it
must have been asleep in some corner of the window or
in one of the deep pleats of this curtain . . . that hangs
in front of the window, perpendicular and immobile.'
In this 'profound and total silence' – we should reflect
on this distinction – the door, all of a sudden, gently
opens and Alberte appears, terrified she may have made
a noise.[20]

Another bedroom imagined as impregnated with
silence is that of the young woman bent over her work
who is so feelingly described by Victor Hugo. Work,
purity, piety and quiet coexist in her attic. In this

'obscure refuge', while 'musing on God, simple and without fear, this maiden performed her noble and worthy task, dreamy Silence was seated at her door'.[21] The voices on the wind, which 'rose vaguely from the silent doorsteps' of the street, say to her: 'Be pure! . . . Be calm . . . Be joyful . . . Be good.'[22]

Angelique, the heroine of Zola's *The Dream*, a novel in which a permanent silence contrasts with the sound of the nearby cathedral bells, seems to illustrate the Hugolian dream. Silence is crucial to one of the novel's great scenes: on the evening when, for the first time, the lovesick Félicien appears, the silence in the bedroom was 'so absolute' that it accentuated every sound and revealed the noises 'of the quivering, sighing house', the noises that inspire night terrors.[23]

Jules Verne, in a comic short story with the title *A Fantasy of Dr Ox*, pushed his description of the total silence that reigned within an imaginary Flemish town to absurd extremes, which allowed him to itemize all the noises that would ordinarily have been heard. Thus the residence of the Burgomaster van Tricasse was a 'peaceful and silent' mansion, 'whose doors never creaked, whose windows never rattled, whose floors never groaned, whose chimneys never roared, whose weathercocks never grated, whose furniture never squeaked, whose locks never clanked, and whose occupants never made any more noise than their shadows'. The god Harpocrates, he adds, would assuredly have chosen it for his Temple of Silence.[24]

The French novelist of the next century who was obsessed by the silence of the bedroom and driven to describe it and convey it was undoubtedly Georges Bernanos. This is particularly visible in his *Monsieur*

Ouine. The quality of the silence of this man's bedroom reflects his character, 'genius of nothingness', of emptiness and of evil, 'schoolteacher of nothingness', 'pederast of souls', monstrous reptile. Here, silence expresses desperation. It accompanies a death, preceded by a long last agony.

The young Steeny, when he first enters Monsieur Ouine's room, is at once struck by 'the wondrous silence of the little bedroom, softly turning on an unseen axis'. He even thinks he can feel it 'slipping across his forehead, over his chest and along his palms, caressing him like water'.[25] He then becomes aware of a murmur, a distant weeping. 'One could not say that the silence was broken, but it did flow by him, little by little going on its way.' Behind him, there was 'a scarcely perceptible shudder', which was not yet a noise, but which preceded and foreshadowed one.[26]

Later, Monsieur Ouine talks of Anthelme, his landlady's husband, who was on his deathbed.

> He spoke calmly, deliberately, in a voice hardly lowered at all, yet [Steeny], not without a vague sense of fear, thought he felt that they were enclosed within the same silence, a silence absorbing only the higher registers of sound and leaving the illusion of becoming itself some sort of audible purity.[27]

In fact it was Monsieur Ouine, who was himself a silence that poisoned minds and corrupted instincts. This was evident when he was on the point of death: 'Monsieur Ouine's breathing did not disturb the silence of the little room, but just gave it a sort of funereal, almost religious, dignity.'[28] 'For the length of my solitary life', the dying man confides, 'I've [never] been one to talk to myself, in the proper sense of the expression, but I rather spoke in order to avoid hearing myself.' The silence that followed 'brought no relaxation. It was a silence full of other words, unpronounced words, which Steeny thought he heard hissing and twisting in the shadows like a tangle of snakes.' And then, as he died, Monsieur Ouine laughed softly, a sound that 'scarcely even rose above the silence'.[29]

It would be quite inadequate to restrict my discussion to the bedroom as refuge, confinement, fear, the osmosis of silence and the vague susurration of noises coming from outside. A consideration of the silence of bedrooms must also include their furniture, and the objects and even people who have a particular affinity with the silence of these spaces.

The silent discourse of the objects that constitute decor has been called the 'mute language of the soul'.[30] 'Every object', wrote Max Picard

> has a hidden fund of reality that comes from a deeper source than the word that designates the object. Man can meet this hidden fund of reality only with silence. The first time he sees an object, man is silent of his own accord. With his silence, man comes into relationship with the reality in the object which is there before ever language gives it a name. Silence is his tribute of honour to the object.[31]

The object 'speaks', says Georges Rodenbach; 'it expresses its nature in a silent discourse, private because perceptible by its interlocutor alone'. In his poetry, Rodenbach exalted many objects which speak silently to the soul. They include the 'thin window panes always complicit with the outside', against which women press their faces, on Sundays, gazing on emptiness and silence;

the mirror, 'sister soul of the bedroom'; old chests; 'the bronze statuette with arching back, reflecting in a silent hymn'. Here, dreams hang in the air like balloons, and 'the bedroom remains silent and juggles' with them. When evening falls, only the gently vibrating chandelier 'emits its discontented noise in the enclosed silence'. Rodenbach sees the bedroom as a 'regalia of silence with motionless fabrics'. Here more than anywhere else 'the pensive virginity of silence' reigns.

There are many other objects that speak silently to the soul: the bedside lamp; the old portraits 'with which we often converse in silence'; the fish tank, a vessel which communicates a rejection of exteriority, where the water flees 'to the bottom of its house of glass'; and, among the jewels, the pearl, 'being without being'. Rodenbach saw grey as the sensitive colour of silence, together with the white of the plumage of the swans of the canals of Bruges and the black of night. Bedrooms, he wrote:

. . . vraiment sont de vielles gens
Sachant des secrets, sachant des histoires . . .
Qu'elles ont cachés dans les vitres noires
Qu'elles ont cachés au fond des miroirs.

[. . . are really old people / Knowing secrets, knowing stories . . . / Which they have hidden in the black panes / Which they have hidden at the back of the mirrors.]

And night-time see 'a cascade of secrets that no one tells'.[32]

If decor is the silent language of the soul, silence itself imposes on the soul its subtle omnipresence. This is what gives a particular object its aura, that 'boundary where being becomes absence', which then constitutes 'like a subtle vibration, a silent speech'.

Certain beings have an affinity with silence, in particular children. As we have seen, they sense its motherly presence. 'The child', wrote Max Picard, 'is like a little hill of silence', on which 'suddenly the word appears . . . more silence than sound comes out through the words of children.'[33] Many film directors have made children's silence telling. For Philippe Garrel, children induce silence and turn it into territory.[34]

Max Picard dwells on the 'dense silence' that is in animals. They 'carry silence around with them on behalf of man', he wrote, 'and are always putting silence down in front of man.' They are 'images of silence'. But the silence of animals is 'a heavy silence. Like a block of stone'; they try 'to tear themselves away but [are] always chained to it'.[35] Among animals, the cat in particular inhabits the silence it seems to symbolize, a feature that film directors have used to good effect.

Some buildings, too, are temples of silence, though in a different way from the house, its passages and its bedrooms. The most notable are churches and cloisters. 'Cathedrals are built around . . . silence', wrote Max Picard; 'the silence of a Romanesque cathedral exists as a substance . . . it is as though the cathedral, by the very fact of its existence, were producing walls of silence, cities of silence, men of silence.' Cathedrals, he continues, 'are like silence inlaid with stone . . . [they] stand like enormous reservoirs of silence.'[36]

Huysmans, especially in his novels of conversion, keeps presenting his heroes as searching for silence, anxious to seek refuge in it, attracted in particular by that found in 'deserted churches and dark chapels'. Durtal, living in Lourdes and renouncing the ugly modern basilica, takes pleasure in frequenting the old and now derelict church: 'Very silent, hardly lighted at all, and very intimate, it was almost empty on weekdays' and, having emerged from the crowds of the new Lourdes, he loved 'to take refuge there'. The handful of women who prayed in front of the holy sacrament remained motionless in their seats and noiseless; not a sound was to be heard; here, 'you could talk to [the Virgin] sweetly and at length in the silence and the dimness'.[37]

Durtal went to live in Chartres in order to enjoy the cathedral, which he expected to find a haven of silence. When, on his first visit, he descended into the crypt, his hopes were only partly satisfied: 'Presently, the clap-clap of sabots became audible, and then the smothered footfall of nuns; there was silence but for sneezing and nose-blowing stifled by pocket handkerchiefs, and then all was still.'[38] Having retreated to a study opposite the towers of the cathedral, and obsessed by the building, he could hear only 'the cawing of the rooks and the strokes of the hours' as 'they fell one by one on the silence of the deserted square'. He had placed his table in front of the window, and 'there he sat dreaming, praying, meditating, making notes', in the 'provincial' silence in which, he believed, he could work better than in Paris. Durtal remained in Chartres for some time, captivated by the tranquil charm of the cathedral close, while also regretting that its silence was only partial. When he decided to leave, it was 'that very silence, that solitude in the cathedral' that he regretted.[39]

While in Chartres, he visited the convent of the Sisters of Saint Paul. There, in the silent corridors, 'the backs of the good women might be seen crossed by the triangular fold of linen, and the click could be heard of their heavy black rosaries on links of copper, as they rattled on their skirts against the hanging bunch of keys'.[40]

I will pass quickly over the connection between silence and the liturgy, it is so self-evident. Durtal emphasizes it, of course, in connection with the movements of the altar boy, which punctuated the service.

> [It] proceeded slowly, soaking into the abject silence of the worshippers, and the child, more reverent and attentive than ever, rang the bell; it was like a shower of sparks tinkling under the smoky vault, and the silence seemed deeper than ever behind the kneeling boy.[41]

The roll call of silent buildings is long and it would be tedious to enumerate them all. They include prisons, where silence is obligatory. Edmond de Goncourt, haunted by the memory of his brother Jules, who had died of aphasia, devoted the second part of his novel *La Fille Élisa* to the destruction of the person by the silence of the penitentiary. Albert Camus takes up the same theme in the last pages of *The Outsider*. Obermann, hero of Senancour's novel of that name, takes refuge in the Bibliothèque nationale in order to overcome the intolerable boredom that afflicts him in Paris. There, he declares, 'I experience greater tranquillity among persons who are silent like myself, than when alone amidst a boisterous crowd'. The library had a peaceful grassy courtyard, with a few statues, and he rarely left, he said, 'without pausing for a few minutes in this hushed enclosure'.[42]

Let us return now to Julien Gracq's *The Opposing Shore*, which, as already observed, is a work in which every nuance of silence plays its part. The Admiralty, the fortress in which the narrator is based, has the silence of an abandoned hulk, and this 'was the sign of an arrogant hostility'. The building is inhospitable from beginning to end of the novel. 'The silence of its empty casemates, of its corridors buried like mine galleries in the dread density of stone', gave it 'the dimensions of a dream'.

The heart of this silence was in the map room, to which the author keeps returning. At the beginning of the novel, the silence of this room is 'cloistral'; inside it, at the same time, it was as if 'something had mysteriously awakened'. From the main map, over which the narrator pored for hours on end, there appeared to come 'a faint rustling', which 'seemed to people the enclosed room and its lurking silence'. This oppressive place, in which the idea was first conceived of confronting the enemy, long dormant, by an expedition on the ship *The Redoubtable*, seemed an oasis of silence. The narrator, hero of the foolhardy venture, returned from his foray to the calm of his absent commander's office, where now, in the 'muffled silence', there could be heard the lapping of the sea, and in the distance the sound of a machine 'wakening that secluded silence like the murmur of bees'.[43] The quiet of the Admiralty's rooms now reflected the defiance triggered in him by the decision.

Places and sounds weigh on people; behaviour and choices feel its subtle influence. These impressions have marked so many authors that they have constantly returned to them, and evocations of space have become an expression of their inner state. Nature, too, would excite their senses and stimulate their quest for silence.

2

The Silences of Nature

Certain sounds, said Maurice de Guérin, make silence resonate, while also giving depth to space. Memories, in the form of reminiscences, then start to speak in the inner silence. On 14 August 1833, he wrote:

> an immense motionless veil, without a single fold, covers the whole face of the sky . . . favoured by this silence, every sound arising from the faraway fields reaches the ear – the songs of the labourer, the voices of children, chirping and the peculiar cries of animals, and from time to time a dog barking I know not where . . . a great silence reigns, and I hear, as it were, the voices of a thousand sweet and touching recollections, which arise in the far-off past and come murmuring to my ear.[1]

For Leconte de Lisle beams of light were 'the sparkling silence of the skies'.[2] Mallarmé, on the other hand, wanted the accumulating banks of fog to rise and build 'a great silent ceiling'.[3] However, it is probably Henry David Thoreau who has most carefully analysed the more general link that connects silence to the things of nature. 'The human soul', he said, 'is a silent harp in God's quire.'[4] When he walked in the woods and in the countryside, he felt that

> all sound is nearly akin to Silence; it is a bubble on her surface which straightway bursts . . . it is a faint utterance of Silence, and then only agreeable to our auditory nerves when it contrasts itself with the former. In proportion as it does this, and is a heightener and intensifier of the Silence, it is harmony and purest melody.[5]

This led him to conclude: 'Silence alone is worthy to be heard. Silence is of various depth and fertility, like soil.'[6] Seeking greater precision, he analysed the effect of hay on silence, and the nature of the silence of mosses. Having stopped in the barn on Baker Farm, he sat 'rustling the hay', and observed that 'the crackling of the hay makes silence audible';[7] and in his 'Natural history of Massachusetts', he records how he contemplated the mosses so as to appreciate 'the beauty there is in [them]', because their life was 'silent and unambitious'.[8]

Once settled at Walden, deep in the country and close to the woods, Thoreau smiled at the good fortune that enabled him to analyse the host of small noises that both revealed the silence and created it. For there could be no silence unless it was broken by the infinitude of sounds of nature, of birds, of frogs, even of leaves. At Walden, there was no need to search for silence, it was everywhere. But, 'if we would enjoy the most intimate society with that in each other's which is without, or above', then 'we must . . . be silent'.[9]

Max Picard, in the twentieth century, felt very much the same. 'The things of nature', he wrote, 'are filled with silence. They are like great reserves of silence.' The weather itself was impregnated with a special silence; each season came from the silence of the season that preceded it. In winter, 'silence is visible'; in spring, 'it is as if the green had passed silently from one tree to another'.[10]

Similarly, certain film directors have shown themselves alert to the silence of the quotidian, which some of them have tried to convey. Nicolas Klotz says that good films are silent, while adding that 'being silent is by no means the same thing as not talking'. He regrets that more and more films today do not talk but that increasingly few are silent. Silence, he says, 'is where the world begins', but today it frightens people.[11] Jean Breschand, appealing for silence, calls it 'the non-rupture' of a 'sweet audible *continuum*, of the ambient familiar babble', of the 'background noise of daily life'. For him, silence is an ambience, a 'sweet, soft and continuous sound', and anonymous.[12]

Let us follow these general considerations by looking more closely at the times and the places in nature in which particular types of silence can be felt. The obvious place to begin is with the relationship between night – or, to be more precise, night-time – and silence. Lucretius, in the *De rerum natura*, evoked 'night's austere silence', which is omnipresent. At the end of the eighteenth century, Joseph Joubert saw this time 'as a great text of silence'.[13] Maurice de Guérin dwelled on the moment when night falls and 'silence enfolds me'. Then the wind drops, the copses become still and 'the noise of man, always the last to be hushed', fades into the distance. 'The universal hum ceases', and all that remains is the faint scratching of his pen writing in the nocturnal silence.[14]

Chateaubriand associated the still of night with the effect of the moon:

The Silences of Nature

When the first silence of night and the last murmurs of day struggle for the mastery on the hills, on the banks of the rivers, in the woods and in the valleys; when the forests have hushed their thousand voices; when not a whisper is heard among the leaves; when the moon is high in the heavens, and the ear of man is all attention.[15]

It is then that a bird begins to sing and reveals the silence of the night. In his *Contemplations,* Victor Hugo wrote:

Je suis l'être incliné . . .
Qui demande à la nuit le secret du silence.[16]
[I am the bowed creature . . . / Who demands from night
the secrecy of silence.]

Across the Atlantic, Walt Whitman proclaimed 'the splendour of silence' and evoked the 'still, nodding . . . mad, naked summer night'.[17]

Georges Rodenbach, too, kept returning in his poetry to the connection between night, the moon and silence. He added the night-time presence of the water of the river and the canals of Bruges as it slept 'in heavy silences'. Here, night 'set out its silent jewels, on this water tormented by regret'.[18]

Gaston Bachelard has emphasized how night amplifies the aural resonances that compensate for the obliteration of colour. The ear is thus the sense of night-time. While shapes become indistinct at dead of night, noises are enshrined in the silence and reach the ear in an imperceptible fashion.[19]

In the twentieth century, Proust lingered over the quality of the silence of moonlight. Legrandin, on his terrace, waxes lyrical about the silence and its shadow: '[T]here comes in all lives a time . . . when the weary eyes can endure but one kind of light, the light [of] a fine evening ... when the ears can listen to no music save what the moonlight breathes through the flute of silence.'[20] It is at dead of night, anchored to its substance, said Valéry, that the spirit, remarkably alone, distinct and rested, feels illuminated by the shadows, and 'the silence speaks to it at close range'.[21] When dawn breaks, the soul senses that 'the first murmurings in the space that grows light settle on the silence', and the coloured shapes that emerge are 'superposed on shadows'.[22]

It is probably Philippe Jaccottet who, in our own day, has most perceptively described the sensations that link the moon and silence. At first, he says, he was frightened by the almost total silence existing out of doors at dead of night.[23] On 30 August 1956, around three a.m., when the rising moon shone on his bed and the silence was total, and he could hear absolutely nothing, no wind, no birds, no traffic, he was gripped by a terrible dread. 'Before this silent and empty immobility', he felt fear and longed for the 'arrival of light'. By contrast, one moonlit night, silence seemed to be another name for describing space. The night star transformed the earth, and made it freer, more transparent, more intimate. It conferred such tranquillity and immobility on the landscape that you could hear 'the silent breathing of the leaves'.[24]

I shall begin my discussion of the places where silence has a particular importance with the desert, site of silence par excellence. I shall evoke the experience of the Desert Fathers at a later stage. Sadly for our purposes, we lack the evidence that would let us know what they felt in the face of this space, other than in relation to their search for God. By contrast, from the nineteenth century, we have major texts that describe the emotional experience of individuals confronted with the silence of the desert. In France, Chateaubriand, Lamartine, Fromentin, Nerval, Flaubert and then, from the inter-war years, travellers seeking adventure and participants in the colonization of the deserts, of whom there were many, all described the feelings they experienced when they had been entombed in this space.

Chateaubriand, who seized 'the Orient by the ear', depicted the desert as a vast silence of desolation born of despotism.[25] He believed that the political system petrified people and the world. Already, in Constantinople, the silence was continuous; 'no sound of carts or carriages' could be heard. There were no bells and few trades employing hammers, and 'you see around you a crowd of mutes'. To which was added, in his imagination, the silence of the seraglio. The executioner himself, who strangled with a silken thread, was silent. In this Empire, silence was a condition of survival. Alexandria, too, was cruelly silent. Chateaubriand had already experienced the silence of the despotic Orient as he travelled through Greece. In the ruins of Sparta, 'the silence around me was profound'. Here, silence signified the slavery and death of the spirit of ancient Greece. In short, the Orient seemed to Chateaubriand to be threatened by both 'abandonment and neglect'.[26]

In Jerusalem, which dominated its desert setting, Chateaubriand invested the silence with a very different meaning, contrasting it with the silence born of despotism. In Judea, 'a land wrought by miracle', the desert 'still seems mute with terror, and seems as if it has not dared to break the silence since the Eternal one'.[27] But here the desert was first and foremost the place where the word of God was heard. Its silence was not that of the humiliation or the despondency produced by despotism but rather a sign of the ineffable presence of God. It was a presentiment of the silence which would precede the last trump and the sounds of the heavenly Jerusalem.

Through these images and sensations, Chateaubriand provides an introduction to the particularities of desert space. Pure, atopic, amorphous, anomic, constructed of minerality, of immensity, of total sterility and of emptiness, it stimulated transcendent dreams and imparted the sense of infinity. However, it was at the same time deadly, because it was an 'allusive and metaphoric' representation of eternity.[28] It made the world unreal. This was what the silence of the desert conveyed for the nineteenth-century traveller.

Guy Barthélemy sees in the musings of Lamartine on the desert, which are rich in traces of the presence of God, the taste of the Romantics for spatial representations of infinity. The aesthetic of the sublime here often shapes the representation of the desert, a 'purifying machine', which enables people to rediscover an authenticity in the drastic separation from their peers, and to engage in a reinvention of the self. This is why, here, silence is essential.[29]

> Ainsi, dans son silence et dans sa solitude,
> Le désert me parlait mieux que la multitude.
> O désert! ô grand vide où l'écho vient du ciel!
> Parle à l'esprit humain, cet immense Israël!
> . . .
> Dans ce morne désert converser face à face
> Avec l'éternité, la puissance et l'espace:
> Trois prophètes muets, silences pleins de foi,

Qui ne sont pas tes noms, Seigneur! mais qui sont toi,
Evidences d'esprit qui parlent sans paroles.

[So, in its silence and in its solitude, / The desert spoke to
me more than the multitude. / O desert! O great emptiness
where the echo comes from heaven! / Speak to the human
spirit, this immense Israel! . . . [and may I] In this mournful
desert, speak face-to-face / With eternity, power and space;
/ Three mute prophets, silences full of faith, / Who are not
your names, Lord! But who are you, / Evidences of a mind
that speak without words.]

Something similar was said, though with less talent,
by Félicien David in his 'ode-symphony', 'Le Désert',
with words by Auguste Colin:

Au désert, tout se tait; et pourtant, ô mystère!
Dans ce calme silencieux
L'âme pensive et solitaire
Entend des sons mélodieux
Ineffables accords de l'éternel silence![30]

[In the desert, everything is quiet; and yet, O mystery! / In
this silent calm / The pensive and solitary soul / Hears sweet
sounds, / Ineffable harmonies of eternal silence!]

Deep in the desert, adds Barthélemy, 'the infinite is
revealed, and silence is a part of this revelation, first as
expression of the hollowing out and dematerialization
of the world, then as paradoxical, oxymoronic and even
mysterious access to this infinite mystery'. The soul is
bathed in the 'ineffable chords of eternal silence' where
'each grain of sand has its voice'.[31]

Eugène Fromentin, poet, painter and great connois-
seur of the desert, as he felt it and expressed it in his

painting, but also, and of particular relevance for us, in his *Un été dans le Sahara* (*A Summer in the Sahara*), presents a world of sensations in which silence is fundamental. It is a 'spatial exaltation of nothingness', site of an 'aesthetic of disappearance'.

Guy Barthélemy has magnificently described the specificity of the silence of the desert. In this *vastitas*, where every sense is disrupted, 'silence too is something Other'. In the desert 'you can no longer consider silence as the opposite of noise, but you are brought to see it as a *state* which introduces you to another dimension of the real that is immediately internalised . . . which creates a new relationship to reality'.[32]

The emptiness of the desert, 'inexhaustible reservoir of novel sensations', 'unlocks the unknown world of infinitely small noises', in other words, paradoxically, the immensity of the desert introduces us to the infinitesimally tiny. For Fromentin, 'silence is one of the most subtle charms of this solitary and empty land',[33] because it is born of emptiness and acquires a density that encourages a spiritual interpretation. Here, sounds evaporate in the silence. It is an essential element in the emotionalism of the desert. Fromentin's *Un été dans le Sahara* is full of descriptions of silence. 'The silence around me is intense', he wrote from D'jelfa to a friend who had remained in Paris.

> The silence communicates to the soul an equilibrium unknown to you, who have lived in the tumult: far from oppressing you, it inclines you to light thoughts. People think it represents the absence of noise just as darkness represents the absence of light: this is a mistake. If I may compare aural sensations to those of sight, the silence that

reigns over vast spaces is more a sort of aerial transparency, which gives greater clarity to the perceptions, unlocks the unknown world of infinitely small noises, and reveals a range of inexpressible delights.[34]

In the desert, there is always the same silence, 'a sort of impassivity which seems to have descended from on high into things'. It is significant that progress in the desert is always made 'in the most profound silence'.[35]

Flaubert, on his travels in Egypt, failed to engage in a thoughtful analysis of the silence. It plays only a very small role in his account, mentioned on at most nine occasions. The observations in his *Voyage en Égypte* are visual, olfactory or tactile. This unwillingness to write about the silence has puzzled critics. His interests lay elsewhere, said Pierre-Marc de Biasi.[36] For Flaubert, the desert was primarily experienced through the body. It was not a place for the projection of states of mind, and expression was deliberately limited to the strict minimum.

Saint-Exupéry is probably the best twentieth-century example of those writers who have described their experience of the desert and its silence. 'Over the desert', he wrote, 'a vast silence as of a house in order' reigns.[37] The silence in the desert was composed of a thousand silences. When an aircraft flew over, the engine made a 'dense all-engulfing sound behind which the landscape [streamed] by in silence, like a film'.[38] In the experience of this airman, the deepest silence was that of the telephone line signalling the loss of an aeroplane and its pilot.[39]

The taste for mountains, like that for the sea, spread in the eighteenth century with the rise of the cult of the sublime. It was associated in the experience of travellers and in their imaginary with rocks, stones, snow and ice, inevitably, but also with silence. In his *Voyages dans les Alpes* (*Travels in the Alps*), Horace-Bénédict de Saussure acclaimed 'the repose and profound silence' of the summits at night, but confessed to having been overcome by a 'kind of terror'.[40]

Senancour's Obermann, staying in Fribourg, found none of the 'still sounds' he would have wished to hear when 'vagueness' was 'brooding over the earth'.[41] For, since infancy, 'wants with no limit devoured me in silence'.[42] However, when he discovered the Alps he recognized 'this preconceived Nature'. For, he wrote, 'in the presence of the silence of the chalets', seeing 'the reflections of the moon . . . I hearkened to the sound of another world'.[43] Everything was silent except 'a torrent rolling profoundly through dense forest land in the heart of the silence'. The impressions which caused this melancholy related to this silence. 'The days escape from the silence',[44] like the water falling from the cascade. In the mountains, the sombre gorges 'were voiceless'; they will be silent forever, and he realized 'in the silence that to-morrow all things on earth may end'.[45]

That said, the sensations he experienced suggested to Obermann, elsewhere, a series of hymns to the silence of the mountains, its silent brooks, the 'solemn silence of the great valleys', and the silence that came at night as darkness fell; the noise of the waterfalls seemed, paradoxically, only to add to 'the unchanging silence of the high peaks and the glaciers and the night'. Also in the mountains were two flowers, which, he said, 'seem to bloom in silence and almost devoid of fragrance', but by which 'I am more attracted than I can say': the field-barbel (cornflower) and even more the early Easter daisy, 'the meadow marguerite'.[46]

Even beyond works of fiction, we find throughout the nineteenth century the same appreciation of the silence of the mountains, to the point where it can become wearisome. At the end of this period, John Muir, indefatigable explorer of, among others, the heights of the Sierra Nevada, describes his ascent of Mount Shasta, where the snow fell in flakes which settled noiselessly in the dry air: 'to be sleeping alone in the mountains on a calm night and to feel the touch of the first of these little silent messages from heaven is a memorable experience: no one could forget something so delicate'.[47]

This text prompts us to associate the silence of the mountains with that of snow, the 'sweet beguiler', Rodenbach's 'pensive sister of silence', who encourages a retreat into an interior world. 'How abundant is the snow!' he wrote:

Elle est silencieuse. On peut
Lui confier tout ce qu'on veut;
C'est une sûre confidente.[48]

[It is silent. You can tell it anything you want; it is a trusty confidant.]

Zola's A Love Affair contains one of his most beautiful passages, in which he describes the silence of the snow falling in the cemetery where Mme Rambaud has been praying over the grave of her daughter:

... the endlessly shifting layers of whiteness grew thicker, like floating gauzes gradually unwinding. The snow fell ... without the sound of a sigh ... the flakes ... alighted one by one, ceaselessly, in their millions, more silently than a flower sheds its petals; and this moving multitude, whose march through space could not be heard, brought an oblivion of earth and of life, a sense of sovereign peace.[49]

In Plato's *Euthydemus* there is a vain debate between a sophist and his interlocutors in which silence is opposed to speech. The conclusion is that things, in particular stones, are silent but also speak. These, we may conclude, are materialized and loquacious silences.[50]

Michelet sought out the melancholy of the mountains, but did not anticipate, he admits, the gloomy silence. On the banks of the Swiss Rhine, in the lapiaz, there were no more flowers, only stones and deep silence: the route was 'doleful'. Here, 'the process of erosion is the more successfully accomplished in silence, to reveal, one morning, a desert of hideous nakedness, where nothing shall ever again revive'.[51] Here, the silent work of nature results in devastation, erosion 'deficient both in the desire and capability of good', whereas in the Southern Seas, he wrote, the 'silent toil of the innumerable polyps' creates 'the future Earth; on whose surface, perhaps, Man shall hereafter reside'.[52]

The sea, too, was a silent world, with a character all its own. 'The serenity of the ocean fills you with pleasure', wrote Chateaubriand in the *Genius of Christianity*, 'and you admire the silence of the abyss, because it arises from the very profundity of its waters.'[53] Joseph Conrad, in *The Shadow Line*, makes his readers feel the calamitous nature of the dead calm of the tropical high seas and its terrible silence. It was all of a piece, in these parts, with 'the brooding stillness of the world'.[54] It was a mirror of despair. On board, hours passed without the slightest sound being heard, and the captain envisaged the end of the ship and death in this absolute calm. 'When the time came', he thought, 'the blackness would overwhelm silently the bit of starlight falling upon the ship, and the end of all things would for come without a sigh, stir, or murmur.'[55]

Manoeuvres were performed noiselessly, as if the sailors were no more than ghosts overwhelmed by a dreadful lethargy. Total silence went with total immobility. There was 'a deadly stillness', a silence 'so profound that you could have heard a pin drop' on deck. Around the ship, however, was 'the indolent silence of the sea',[56] an implicit reference to the hell whose image sets the novel's tone, a reworking of the trope of the Phantom Ship.

On the high seas, as evening comes, the porpoises emerge and then flee, wrote Albert Camus in 'La mer au plus près, Journal de bord' (The Sea Close By. Logbook), leaving behind 'the silence and anguish of primitive waters'.[57] But this sombre emotion differed from that evoked in him by dawn at Tipasa: '

> In this light and this silence ... I listened to an almost forgotten sound within myself ... and awake now, I recognized one by one the imperceptible sounds of which the silence was made up: the figured bass of the birds, the sea's faint, brief sighs at the foot of the rocks, the vibration of the trees, the blind singing of the columns, the rustling of the wormwood plants, the furtive lizards. I heard that; I also listened to the happy torrents rising within me.[58]

The evocative power of the coastal woods heard by Camus is also found deep in the forest. Max Picard described the forest as 'like a great reservoir of silence out of which the silence trickles in a thin, slow stream and fills the air with its brightness'.[59] In the American forest, at night, observed Chateaubriand, when the camp fire begins to die down, 'one would say that silences follow upon silences. I seek vainly to hear in a universal tomb some noise betraying life'.[60] After a tree had fallen, making the forests 'bellow', the 'noises weaken and die in almost imaginary distance'. At one in the morning, the wind has 'awakened sounds' and 'the aerial music begins anew'.[61] Chateaubriand's imagination then conjured up a powerful image which conveyed 'the deepest silence of the forests' in the midday heat: at this time, the male snake shakes his rattle to call the female; 'this love signal is the only sound which then strikes the traveller's ear'.[62]

Let us now return to the sensations experienced by Henry David Thoreau in woodland. One of the most intense was brought on by his awareness of the silence of plant growth. In winter, he wrote, when frost made the ground 'sonorous' like seasoned wood, 'the jingling of the ice on the trees is sweet and liquid' and the smoke ascends silently. In summer, when the woods are washed of their sins, Nature can silently 'reassert her rule'.[63] Victor Hugo, in *Les Voix intérieures* (*Inner Voices*), gave thanks for those times in forests, in summer when 'silence sleeps on the velvety mosses'.[64]

Émile Moulin, arcane analyst of silence, quotes Sully Prudhomme, who wrote, in *Les Solitudes*:

> Les bois ont donc aussi leur façon de se taire
> Et d'être obscurs aux yeux que le rêve y conduit.
> On sent dans leur silence errer l'âme du bruit.[65]

[So the woods too have their way of being silent / And of being obscure in the eyes turned on them in dreams. / One feels in their silence the spirit of noise roaming.]

John Muir was deeply moved by the giant trees he saw in California, and pondered the silence of the sequoias; age-old, they kept humans at a distance. They spoke only to the winds. They thought only of the sky. They seemed to know nothing, to stand 'solitary, silent and serene'.[66]

In 1920, Robert Walser, walking in a pine forest felt

> it was quiet as in a happy human soul, as in the interior of a temple, as in a palace and enchanted dream-wrapped fairy-tale castle, as in Sleeping Beauty's castle, where all sleep, and all are hushed for centuries of long years . . . So solemn was it in the forest that lovely and solemn imaginings, quite of their own accord, took possession of these sensitive walker there. How glad I was at this sweet forest softness and repose!

Here, a 'slight sound or two' would only intensify 'the prevailing soundlessness, which I inhaled to my very heart's content, and whose virtues I drank and quaffed with due ceremony'.[67]

We now come to the place that is most commonly and frequently visited, whose silence has been most commented on, and which is the most ordinary: the countryside. The silent country walk is a commonplace of self-writing, of the novel and of lyric poetry. In the late eighteenth century, when going for a walk along the footpaths of the grounds of great estates became a ritual, English novelists, Jane Austen and then the Brontë sisters and George Eliot, liked to describe their pleasures. The favourite retreat of St Aubert, in Ann Radcliffe's *The Mysteries of Udolpho*, was a little fishing house, to which he often walked through the countryside with his wife and daughter. He went 'at the sweet evening hour to welcome the silent dusk'.[68]

'Sometimes we walked in silence', says René, in Chateaubriand's novel of that name, describing his country walks with his sister Amélie, 'giving ear to the dull soughing of autumn, or the sound of the dead leaves'. And on Sundays, he reveals, 'leaning against the trunk of an elm, I listened in silence to [the] pious reverberations' of the distant bells.[69] Fromentin's *Dominique* valued the month of October, because it restored silence to the countryside. The historian Guy Thuillier has described the blanket of silence that enveloped the villages of Nivernais in the nineteenth century, awaiting the intermittent and reassuring sounds of arable and pastoral farming being carried on as usual.[70] At this period, the work song, an essential element in the sound world, was meant to attest to the ongoing labours by interrupting the ambient silence. In the total darkness of night, or the solitude of the countryside, the desire to break the silence was also intended to be reassuring.

Victor Hugo, in a poem in his *Inner Voices*, associates Olympio with 'the silent fields' and 'the purity of untrodden grass';[71] and in his ode to trees in *Contemplations*, the speaker who listens to the trees and questions them describes them as 'full of silence'.[72]

Moors are for our purposes archetypal. Barbey d'Aurevilly makes his readers feel the intensity and the specific quality of the silence of the Lande de Lessay. At night it was covered by such a huge cape that, had bandits attacked, it 'would have devoured all the cries that might be cried in its breast'. The narrator, crossing the moor at night with his guide, though neither of them spoke, confides:

What struck me most in all this dense mistiness and darkness was the gloomy mutism of the heavy air. The immensity of the spaces that we were unable to see was revealed by the depth of the silence. This silence, oppressive to both heart and mind, was never once broken during our crossing of this moor, which resembled, said Master Tainnebouy [the guide], *the end of the world*, except, from time to time, by the flapping of the wings of a heron asleep on its legs, but stirred into flight by our approach.[73]

And in his *Un prêtre marié (A Married Priest)*, d'Aurevilly writes that, after Calixte had been buried, 'silence blew in the wind once more and resumed possession of the countryside'.[74]

I have already, discussing the cities of the East, close to the desert, and the patrician residences of Bruges, quoted some extreme examples of the evocation of urban silence. In the case of Bruges, however, I have only skimmed the surface of what has been said of the town itself. Georges Rodenbach saw its silence as associated with night, the old quays, the water of the canals and of the river and, as we have seen, the patrician residences. 'Paths of colourless silence' ran through the heart of the town of Bruges,[75] and 'waters full goodbyes [are here] inert like the silent bandages of a corpse'.[76] In the towns of Belgium:

> . . . on sent un froid silence uniforme qui plane;
> Si despotique, encor qu'il soit débile et las . . .
> Que la moindre rumeur infinitésimale
> Cause un trouble, paraît une chose anormale
> Comme de rire auprès d'un malade qui dort.
>
> Car le silence là vraiment s'atteste! Il règne,
> Il est impérieux, il est contagieux;

Et le moins raffiné des passants s'en imprègne
Comme d'encens dans un endroit religieux . . .
Ah! ces villes, ce grand silence monotone . . .
Ce silence si vaste et si froid qu'on s'étonne
De survivre soi-même au néant d'alentour.[77]

[You feel a silent, uniform, hovering chill; / So despotic, even though stupid and weary . . . / That the least infinitesimal murmur is troubling, seems something abnormal, like laughter round a sleeping invalid. / Because there the silence truly makes itself felt! It reigns, / it is imperious, it is contagious; / and the least sensitive of passers-by is imbued by it / As with incense in a place of worship. / Ah! These towns, this great monotonous silence . . . / This silence so vast and so cold that you are surprised you yourself survive in the surrounding void.]

However, there are other cities that are silent, but in different ways. The French novelists of the nineteenth century liked to portray the silence of small provincial towns, typically seats of bishoprics. Balzac was the first to explore the theme of provincial towns as symbols of past centuries, silent because dead, obsessed with their history, shunning anything modern. Guerande, scene of the first chapters of *Béatrix*, may be seen as a model. The silence that Balzac suggests and frequently refers to permeates his descriptions of the town, the house of the Du Guénic family and the old man who lives there. As soon as you entered Guerande, the silence struck:

A painter, a poet would sit there silently, to taste the quietude which reigns beneath the well-preserved arch of the postern, where no voice comes from the life of the peaceful city . . . The town produces somewhat the same effect upon the mind as a sleeping-draught upon the body. It is silent as Venice.

Every artist and every citizen who passed through Guerande briefly felt the desire, wrote Balzac, to end his days there in silence. The house of the Du Guénic (or Guaisnic) lay 'at the end of a silent, damp, and gloomy lane'. The old master does not speak: 'such silence is a trait of Breton character', utter silence 'is the surest indication of an unalterable will'. It has something granite-like about it. During the evening, which began at six o'clock, 'the silence . . . became so deep' that you could plainly hear 'the clicking of the knitting needles' of the 80-year-old sister of the master of the house, who knitted without pause. When the curé left after visiting the family, you could hear 'the heavy tread' of his 'cautious feet', which only ceased when, in the silent town, 'the closing of the door of the parsonage echoed behind him'.[78]

The episcopal cities huddled round their cathedral in *La Comédie humaine* exemplify these silent towns. In Tours, the abbé Birotteau lives in an apartment, which he sees as highly prestigious, on the ground floor of a house at the end of the rue de la Psalette. This dark, damp and cold house was perpetually 'wrapped in silence, broken only by the bells [or] the call of the jackdaws'. The curé appreciated 'the silence and the peace that reigned' in his study.[79] 'Silence, cold, inaction, egoism', writes Nicole Mozet, typify the Balzacian provincial town; and the characters, such as the abbé Birotteau, are in keeping.[80]

Every reader of Barbey d'Aurevilly will remember the quality of the night-time silence in the square in

Valognes, described at the beginning of *Le Chevalier Des Touches*, as half past eight strikes: only 'the sound of two dragging clogs, which fear or the bad weather seemed to hasten in their uncertain progress, disturbed the silence of the place des Capucins, which was deserted and dreary', just like the 'lande du Gibet' itself, where they hanged people in days gone by.[81]

As for the twentieth century, let us return to the urban silences suggested in Julien Gracq's *The Opposing Shore*. These towns are veritable 'labyrinths of silence', the silence of pestilence, the silence of decay, the silence of menace. The novel ends with a word picture of the feelings experienced in what is called the magical silence of the night-time streets of Orsenna, the sleeping capital through which Aldo roams after leaving the palace:

> Through the night's stillness, beyond the naked walls, faint sounds rose at intervals from the lower city: running water, the rumble of a distant cart – distinct yet intriguing, like the sighs and movements of a restless sleeper, or the occasional cracking of desert rocks contracting in the night's cold.[82]

This word picture is in stark contrast to what has been said, in our own day, by Pierre Sansot, of the avenue de Breteuil, in Paris, enveloped in comfort by its wealth and the quality of its silence![83]

Many writers have emphasized the specific quality of the silence of ruins, which is enough in itself to trigger a plunge into the past they keep alive. Chateaubriand referred to the ruins of Palmyra as the 'abode of silence'. He evokes 'Death, so poetical because of its bordering upon things immortal, so mysterious on account of its silence'.[84] For Max Picard, the sphinx 'remains from the time of the most violent silence, as an image of that silence, still with us today. After all silence has disappeared, it is still with us, always threateningly ready to invade the world of noise.' More generally, he observed that 'the Egyptian statues are absolutely subjugated by the silence: they are prisoners of the silence'.[85]

It was monuments that suggested to Chateaubriand what may be called 'hearing ruins'. He wished to describe and memorialize three great silences of the past: that of the Escorial, that of Port-Royal and that of Soligny. Thus, at La Grande Trappe, he wished to convey 'the silence of the old lake'. No one now could experience or appreciate it as had been possible two centuries before. Chateaubriand felt it and described it. In the middle of the seventeenth century, if not in 1847, 'you found at midday a silence like that of the middle of the night'.[86]

Chateaubriand believed, nevertheless, that Soligny was a place where one might recover the silence of the past, a place where the ear was exceptionally receptive. An archaeological reconstruction of the silence and the sounds was possible because certain present-day sensations had here acquired the status of vestiges. That said, the attempt proved extremely difficult because the silence of the nineteenth century was insidiously haunted by a more recent history, a reordering and a reinterpretation of its significance, the new social value it had assumed, new forms of the receptiveness it expressed, and the altered meaning given to it. An assemblage of recent memories got in the way of an understanding and memorializing of the silence of the past.

Victor Hugo, by contrast, looked forward. In *Inner Voices*, he imagined what a Paris that had been destroyed would look like in three thousand years, and tried to imagine the quality of the silence that would hang over its ruins. He pictured a man sitting on a hill overlooking the city:

Ô Dieu! de quel aspect triste et silencieux
Les lieux où fut Paris étonneront ses yeux![87]

[Oh God! With how sad and silent an aspect / Will the sites where once was Paris amaze his eyes!]

Fernand Khnopff, *Silence*, 1890
This painting shows the importance of silence for the symbolists.
The gloved hand of the model – the artist's sister – enjoins silence.
But it does more: it invites the viewer to retreat from the external world,
and place themselves, so to speak, outside time.

Odilon Redon, *Closed Eyes*, 1890
More than the 'troubled dream' aimed at by the artist, this is a painting
of a woman listening to an interior language, revealed by her closed eyes.

Georges de La Tour, *Saint Joseph the Carpenter*, 1638/1645
Joseph, not one word of whose is recorded in the Scriptures, personifies
the profundity of absolute silence, here shown next to the divinity of Christ.

Arthur Hughes, The Long Engagement, 1859
It is through silence that love is expressed at its most profound.
When lovers remain silent, they devote themselves to each other.

Edgar Degas, *In a Cafe,* **also called** *Absinthe*
Though sitting side by side, the two people seem to be strangers to each other.
One is plunged into an interior silence, the other remains silent,
but still watches the world go by.

Piero della Francesca, *The Madonna of the Parturition*, 1476/1483
Silence goes with maternity because it implies serenity;
this is one of the rare paintings which portrays the pregnant Virgin.

René Magritte, *The Dominion of Light*, 1954
Everything here contributes to the presence of silence. Magritte, as a surrealist,
confuses the light codes and heightens the contrasts.

Edward Hopper, *Gas*, 1940
The man standing by the petrol pumps, and his tiny shop, are lost in the
immensity of the vast Texas silence, a silence which is also waiting.

3

The Search for Silence

Many people have searched for silence; it is an ancient and a universal quest. It pervades the whole of human history: Hindus, Buddhists, Taoists, Pythagoricians and, of course, Christians, Catholic and perhaps even more Orthodox, have felt the need for and the benefits of silence; and this desire has been felt beyond the spheres of the sacred and the religious. I lack the skills, consequently, to describe it in its totality. Yet I cannot completely ignore something that is fundamental to a history of silence in the West. I shall confine myself to certain quests for silence made in the sixteenth and seventeenth centuries. Those who have subsequently felt the desire for silence have referenced them, explicitly or not.

Silence was at this period seen as a necessary precondition for a relationship with God. Meditation, interior prayer, indeed all prayer, required it. Since antiquity, the monastic tradition had transmitted an *ars meditandi* which emerged from the cloisters in the sixteenth century and which then constituted an internal discipline accessible to the laity. Onto this was grafted the ancient moral philosophy, that of Seneca and Marcus Aurelius, for example, with which the humanists were familiar. This led to advocacy of a struggle against distraction, a concentration of the attention, a meditative quest closely dependent on silence. This process, which led to the wide dissemination of the silent *oratio interior* that has been so well described by Marc Fumaroli, is crucial to a history of silence.

In 1555, the Jesuit father Balthazar Alvarez wrote a treatise with the title *Tratado de la oración de silencio*. He believed that the *oración de la presencia de Dios*, the 'prayer of the presence of God', made it possible to accede to the *oración de silencio*, 'the prayer of silence': 'Then, in the heart, everything is silent, nothing disturbs it, it is the silence in which one hears only the voice of God who instructs and reveals'; this is why one must welcome him 'in silence and in tranquillity'.[1]

The Dominican Luis de Granada proposed a method of inner prayer which would influence people as diverse as Charles Borromeo and Philip Neri, founder of the Oratory. It consisted of imagining an 'inner, silent picture' of the 'visible and tangible features of an act in the life of Christ'. 'A veritable conversation between the sinful self and the sacred scene' could then begin, and Christ and the other persons in the picture, by their gestures and their looks, 'silently appeal for a reflection on the self'. Such an inner prayer, constantly repeated, would create, he believed, a habitus of 'silent movements' which would penetrate all actions.[2]

However, it is the thinking of Ignatius Loyola that had the strongest and deepest influence at this period. His message was based on silence. 'God bestows, God trains, God accomplishes his work, and this can only be done in the silence that is established between the Creator and the creature'; 'he who approaches his Creator and Lord and who reaches him', he is someone who lives in silence.[3]

Living in Manresa, in Catalonia, Ignatius Loyola spent seven hours a day in interior prayer. At mealtimes, when he ate with others, his custom was never to speak, although he listened, in order to use what was said by the guests as material for the encounter with God that would follow the meal.[4]

He saw the spiritual exercise as a way of meditating, of praying, of examining one's conscience and of engaging in the 'contemplation of place'. This required silence, which happened naturally during the 'exercise of night'. One example will help us to understand this exercise performed in silence and which allowed the imagination free play: when eating, said Loyola, 'let him imagine he sees Christ our Lord and His disciples at table, and consider how He eats and drinks, how He looks, how He speaks'.[5]

In a long text on the different ways of praying, Ignatius Loyola spelled out how one should match words to breaths in order to achieve consolation and conquer the desolation provoked by evil spirits. These, he said, enter the soul 'with noise and commotion', whereas the good angel enters peacefully and 'silently'.[6]

This brings us to the mystics. John of the Cross, describing the tranquil night, formed of calm and of solitude in God, emphasizes the importance of silence in mystical rapture. 'In the calm and silence of night and in this knowledge of divine light, the soul discovers . . . a certain correspondence with God.' A sublime musical harmony is established, which 'surpasses all the concerts and all the melodies in the world', and this music is called by the soul 'silent music' because it is 'a calm and peaceful knowledge, without sound of voices, and therefore one enjoys the sweetness of the music and the tranquillity of the silence'. Further, 'even though that music is silent to the natural senses and faculties, it is sounding solitude for the spiritual faculties'.[7]

Later, he describes the benefits of contemplation of the 'hidden and secret wisdom of God': '[W]ithout sound of voices ... as in the silence of quietness of night, apart from all that is sensible and natural, God teaches the soul.'[8] In a word, the silence of the spirit is a necessary condition for God to enter the soul. It 'cancels all rational and discursive activity, thereby enabling direct perception of the divine word'.[9]

We may also, in discussing silence and mysticism, consider the experience and writings of St Teresa of Avila, in particular her description of the 'castle of the soul'. Here, God is reached only in silence through the 'ears of the soul', at night.

The Carthusian rule was based on silence and solitude, completed by a specific book-based education. This, writes Gérald Chaix, made it possible to adhere (*inhaere*) to God 'with all one's heart, with all one's soul and with all one's might'.[10] The exterior silence which features in the Carthusian rule and practices is simply a means of reaching an interior silence, that of the mind (*mens*) and of the heart (*cor*). Purged of all worldly imagination, the mind then thinks solely of God. Though only a procedure for attaining this relationship, the exterior silence imposed by the rule, like solitude, must be scrupulously observed. So also must the renunciation of the study of eloquence in favour of reading works that taught silence and devotion. Gérald Chaix concludes that this ideal of solitude and silence, though perfectly adapted to the age of the Reformation and Counter Reformation, was subsequently found increasingly baffling, and the Carthusians appeared 'fools for God'.[11]

In the seventeenth century, as the external world turned away from silence, two notable personalities gave it a major role in the practice of contemplation: Jacques-Bénigne Bossuet and, more radically, the abbot of Rancé, the reformer of la Trappe. The former repeatedly emphasized in his works the grandeur and the necessity of silence. Bossuet based his exhortations on a passage from the Apocalypse: when the angel broke the Seventh Seal, there was a profound silence in heaven and, during it, 'the angels paid tribute to and venerated the supreme majesty of God. What does this mysterious silence which the angels created in heaven mean?' he asked. That 'every creature, whether in heaven or on earth, must hold their peace, and refrain from speech so as to adore and venerate the grandeur of God.' Hence he urged: 'Every so often, be silent, in imitation of the angels';[12] 'you will never regret having remained silent'.[13]

In this exhortation intended for the Ursulines of Meaux, Bossuet maintains: 'It is only in silence and in the avoidance of useless and distracting speech that [God] will visit you through his inspirations and his grace, and that He will make his presence felt within you.'[14] Exhortations of this type were a leitmotif of his preaching. He recalled the words of St James, who asked that everyone be quick to listen and slow to speak.[15]

'There has to be perfect silence and recollection to hear internally the voice of God';[16] and again addressing the Ursulines of Meaux: 'one loses much through the absence of silence',[17] the desire to speak deflects from God. In religious houses, 'the absence of silence leads to all the faults against charity'.[18] Except when responding to Pilate, Jesus, during his Passion, 'maintained a perpetual silence' – imitate him, urged Bossuet. Where does it come from, this intense eagerness to speak, he asked? It prevents introspection.[19]

Vivid examples reinforced these messages. In the 'Second Panegyric upon St Benedict', Bossuet wrote that, in the solitude of the 'horrible and frightful [desert] to which he withdrew, an awful and terrible silence [prevailed], which was interrupted only by the cries of wild beasts'.[20] It was to encourage him to shun the licentiousness of his youth that God gave him 'an uncultivated and uninhabited land, a desert, a silence, a solitude . . . a dark and awful cavern'.[21] Later, St Bernard, having renounced the world at the age of 22, become 'extraordinarily enamoured of secrecy and solitude', reflecting that the Cross had closed the mouth of Jesus, said to himself: 'I will condemn mine to silence'.[22] At Clairvaux, when some monks found the 'long and horrible' silence of the monastery too harsh, Bernard told them that, 'were they to think seriously about the rigorous examination the great Judge would make of their words, they would not have much difficulty in remaining silent'.[23]

In his 'Meditation on Silence', intended for the Ursulines of Meaux, Bossuet is more specific. There were, he believed, three types of silence: 'the silence of rule, the silence of prudence in conversation, and the silence of patience in affliction'.[24] In thirty years, Jesus spoke only once in the Temple. 'If he said not a word, it was to teach us to remain silent.'[25] In the monastic orders, the rule fixed the times and hours of silence. Some even 'maintained a perpetual and profound silence, and never spoke'. The founders of orders had believed 'that silence cut out many sins and faults'. They had also 'foreseen that devotion and the prayerful spirit could not exist without silence'.[26] Silence was necessary, lastly, to maintain charity, peace and union among the brothers and sisters alike. Whoever wished to reform a monastery, he added, must begin with silence and banish the 'desire to communicate'.

To practise the silence of prudence was to avoid the faults against charity, and to demonstrate a 'wise discretion'. To practise the silence of patience was to 'suffer in silence under the eye of God'; because 'it is silence that sanctifies our crosses and our afflictions'.[27] One should to this end reflect on the attitude of Jesus during the flagellation and the crowning of thorns. It had been said that Christ was the 'victim of silence'. He had demonstrated and consecrated this during his Passion.[28] Silence protected against anger, it was the best way to conquer the passion of vengeance and it was a way of overcoming the 'desires of curiosity'; and, Bossuet concluded, 'by faithfully keeping silent, you will be victorious over all your passions'.[29]

At Soligny, the abbot of Rancé introduced and insisted on silence, to which he devoted his 29th constitution. Many messages of Bossuet echoed the views of Rancé, his friend. The abbot believed that silence went with solitude, which would, without it, be vain. Silence was part of the spirit of penitence and it sanctioned separation from men. It was a sign of rupture and detachment. It was a precondition for forgetting the self, proof that bodily concerns had been put aside. Above all, silence was a precondition for prayer, it was a preparation for listening to the divinity. It facilitated spiritual exercises and access to other languages than speech: that of the interior, that of the hereafter, that of the angels.

Rancé also argued that silence favoured meditation on the vanities. It made it easier to measure on a daily basis the passage of time. It anticipated the silence of the tomb. It prepared, consequently, for eternity, which wiped out time. It was this that made Chateaubriand regard the silence of Rancé as terrible, in its length and its depth. On the point of death, the abbot cried: 'I have only a few moments to live; the best use of them I can make is to pass them in silence.'[30] He was true to his word.

This brings us to the vanitas paintings which were produced in large numbers in the seventeenth century. They are an expression of the powerful presence at this period of meditation on life, death and eternity, performed in silence. Vanitas paintings, writes Alain Tapié, are melancholic in the North, in the aftermath of the *devotio moderna*, and passionate and ecstatic in the South. They are intended to demonstrate or at least remind that life is a dream, and to emphasize the insubstantiality and nothingness of living beings. These canvases, which express in their own way an anticipatory mourning, display a number of recurring motifs, and include many still lifes which show Nature at rest, calm and silent. The aim of vanitas painting was both to shock and to preach by its silence.[31]

The comparative merits of silence and of service,

that is, of the contemplative ideal and the practice of the apostolate, were much argued over in the Middle Ages. The debate had its origins in the passage in the gospel describing the visit of Jesus to Martha and Mary. Martha spoke and busied herself, Mary remained silent and thoughtful. This posed a dilemma for Christians. 'Was it better to remain silent at the feet of the Lord, in contemplation of an intimacy nourished by his presence and his word, or to expend one's energy on many tasks to serve him, both him and his associates?'[32] According to Luke, Jesus appeared to favour the former, given that he said, 'Mary has chosen the better part, which will not be taken away from her', an attitude on Christ's part that once again valorized silence.

The debate was never settled. To the monks fell the part of Mary, to the secular clergy that of Martha, that is, the labours of the active life. That said, the part of Mary often seemed the better of the two: the contemplative life and its silence appeared superior in that they were oriented towards the ultimate end and attained their fulfilment in eternal life. Nevertheless, often, as in the case of the Franciscans, the solution was to alternate between the two positions.[33]

Two centuries later, in 1936, the director Léon Poirier gave his film encapsulating the life of Charles de Foucauld the title L'Appel du silence, not 'du désert' ('The Call of Silence', not 'of the Desert'), which is why I discuss him here rather than in the preceding chapter. After his conversion, Charles de Foucauld stayed for a while in Notre-Dame-des-Neiges, in Ardèche, before spending some time as a novice, a Trappist, at Akbès, in Ottoman Syria. He had long been fascinated by Nazareth, to which he withdrew in 1897, and where he lived in a hut. In short, his religious formation was anchored in two silences, as he himself frequently observed.

In the many spiritual works of Charles de Foucauld, prayer, night and silence are closely linked. One night, soon after his conversion, he felt that Jesus spoke to him. He heard him ask him to begin to live 'with the silent Magdalene, my silent mother and the silent Joseph'.[34] Charles de Foucauld wrote at length about the merits of silence. During his time in Nazareth, Jesus spoke to him again, saying: 'For these thirty years I have instructed you continually, not by words but by my silence.'[35] This makes it easier to understand his ultimate destination. To receive the grace of God, one must pass by way of the desert: '[T]his silence is necessary to the soul.'[36] The call of the desert was for him the call of silence. This conviction is revealed in his correspondence. On 17 July 1901, he wrote to a Trappist: '[I]t is in silence that we love most ardently; noise and words often put out the inner fire; let us be silent . . . like St Magdalen, like St John the Baptist; let us pray God to kindle within us the fire that made their silence and solitude so blessed.'[37] We shall return to Nazareth, as it was experienced by Charles de Foucauld. For the moment, let us note only that, having become a hermit in the Sahara, among the Tuaregs, he settled at Tamanrasset in 1904, where he was assassinated in 1916; he never, during this period, stopped describing the happiness caused by the silence of the desert. In 15 July 1906, for example, he wrote: '[T]his desert is for me deeply sweet . . . so it is hard for me to travel, to leave this solitude and this silence.'[38] He had always wanted, he said, to lead the 'life of Nazareth', a life of solitude and of desert.[39]

The Search for Silence

Orthodox theologians accord silence an even more crucial role than Catholics; sadly, it would take too long to describe their thinking and experience in their full complexity. I will confine myself to a few of their distinctive features. The ineffable peace of Christ is inseparable from silence. The faithful must search for this silence throughout their lives and to achieve it must listen to the voices of the Desert Fathers. As God is unknowable, absolute silence should be maintained in his regard; at most, it is possible to immerse oneself in the silence with which he surrounds himself. Through mystical experience, the soul enters the 'darkness of silence'. Thus a way forward is offered: first to enter one's own soul in silence, to die to the world, then to enter in silence on God, that is, in effect, voluntarily to obscure the intelligence. Of course, monasticism is the best way of accessing this silence, which is a battle against thought, which is renunciation, a forgetting of the self. 'He is silent', wrote Michel Laroche, 'who renounces on this basis [silence], in order to affirm his existence.'[40] Tears often flow in the course of this asceticism, which is why we may define the above by the notion of theology of silence and tears.

It would be highly reductive to restrict the range of quests for silence to those resulting from the desire to assist listening to God and the mystical experience, as the other chapters of this book make clear. Many people have searched for silence outside the religious sphere or on its margins. Many people have shared the opinion expressed by Margaret Parry: '[I]f we wish to achieve an authentic life, it is necessary to construct within us the monastery of silence.'[41] This is a leitmotif in Senancour: it is only 'in the silence of the passions', cried Obermann, that 'it is possible to examine ourselves'.[42] The passages in Thoreau's *Journal* that associate the silence of the woods with the deepening of reflection and of happiness are too numerous to count. In *On the Genealogy of Morality*, Nietzsche observes that it is necessary to be silent to be receptive to new things.

It is probably Maeterlinck who has more than anyone acclaimed the virtues of silence and advocated the search for it; I will return to him at some length in the chapter devoted to the experience of love. Maeterlinck believed that 'transcendence meant death' and that the visible world remains deeply mysterious. At the heart of the inner obscurity, however, throbbed something unknown; it was 'not a great clarity', like that which the great mystics said they saw shine in the depth of night, but 'something unknown, like an enigmatic pledge left us by the Divine Host who comes sometimes and sits in the silence of our night'.[43]

In the twentieth century, Francis Ponge exalted the silence of pine woods as that of a natural cathedral which assists meditation. Today, observes Thierry Laurent, the necessity of silence instructs the work of Patrick Modiano.[44] He presents it as a consolation, says Laurent, as a means of escape to mask despair; hence a quality so precious but so difficult to acquire, that of knowing when to keep silent.

At a simpler, more mundane, level, the quest for silence means a search for silent places. I have already discussed that engaged in by Durtal in the novels of Huysmans (*Là-bas*, *En route*, *La Cathédrale*, *L'Oblat*). And as we have seen, Baudelaire and Proust both engaged in the same search, outside their fiction. In our own day, it is this need that is felt by customers of the French hotel chain, the Relais du silence, which promises its holidaying guests silence, proof of just how precious it has become.

4

The Education and Discipline of Silence

Among the Greeks, the god Harpocrates was repre-
sented with a finger to his lips. With this gesture, he
called for silence. Injunctions to be silent have been
common and commonplace throughout history. They
imply something to be learned, because silence cannot
be presumed. 'Some there are', wrote Maeterlinck,
'that have no silence, and that kill the silence around
them, and these are the only creatures that pass
through life unperceived'; this, he says, is because 'we
cannot conceive what sort of man is he who has never
been silent. It is to us as though his soul were feature-
less.'[1] An education in silence is all the more essential
in that it is the medium within which great things take
shape. For these finally to emerge, therefore, silence
must be learned. 'Hold thy tongue for one day; on
the morrow how much clearer are thy purposes and
duties', said Maeterlinck.[2] Talking, on the other hand,
is only too often the art of stifling and suspending
thought, which can only take place in silence. For all
these reasons, said Maeterlinck, we fear it and spend

a large part of our lives seeking places where it does not reign.

The learning of silence, and even more ways of imposing it, are acts recorded and developed at length in the dictionaries. The *Grand Dictionnaire universel Larousse du XIXe siècle*, for example, lists and comments on the disciplines and failure to observe them: 'to be silent', 'to command silence', 'to ask for silence', 'to impose silence', 'to observe silence' and, *a contrario*, 'to break silence'. At the Byzantine court, notes the author of the entry, the job of the Silentiarios was to ensure silence.

Injunctions to be silent are characteristic of particular places, like churches, educational institutions and the army, and particular situations, where it is a requirement of civility, politeness or submission. Silence is obligatory, even today, not only in churches, temples and mosques, but often in the immediate vicinity of these buildings, too. Inside a church, silence is a mark of respect, of self-control and of the capacity to master the impulses. It makes it easier, as we have seen, to avoid mental distraction and straying thoughts. The religious service is itself a school of silence and the avoidance of agitation. Children must refrain from talking, and even more shouting, inside churches and nearby; and the altar boys, in particular, become accustomed to the bodily control demanded by the staging of the ceremony.

A specific somatic culture here reinforces the requirement for silence. It is demonstrated by the postures of worship and in the procession to the holy table. Since the second half of the nineteenth century the practice of Perpetual Adoration has been a formidable training in silence. The worshipper, often an adolescent or even a child, a pupil in a Catholic college or school, must, alone and in silence, adore the Eucharist exposed in the monstrance in the church or chapel of the institution. This exercise, combining the ability to remain silent and to maintain the correct posture, can last for as long as an hour.

During the mass, but during Vespers, Compline and Benediction of the Blessed Sacrament, too, the signals that punctuate ceremonial time teach the collective orders, indicate the moments of especially profound silence and decree the posture to be adopted. Outside the church, a similar discipline operates during processions. At Corpus Christi, wrote Chateaubriand in the *Genius of Christianity*, the silences, which are numerous, make a deep impression on the faithful. They differ from the 'pious silence' when the Host is raised. 'At intervals the sacred melody ceases, and there reigns only a majestic silence, like that of the vast ocean in a moment of calm. The multitude are bowed in adoration before God; nothing is heard but here and there the cautious footsteps of those who are hastening to swell the pious throng.'[3]

Another conspicuous silence in the manifestations of the Catholic religion is that of the bells between Good Friday and Easter Sunday. Many have testified to the deep feeling to which this gives rise, as also to that caused by the noise announcing the Resurrection. At la Trappe, to mark the exercises, the silencing of the bells made it necessary to resort to the more discreet rattle.

In religious and later secular educational establishments, silence has been imposed since the beginning of modern times. It was seen as a mark of respect towards the head of the institution, a sign of the self-control that wards off misbehaviour and a prerequisite for paying attention. If you are quiet, you can listen properly. Further, as the philosopher Alain observed in 1927, silence is just as contagious as laughter. It is important, therefore, to make sure it triumphs over its rival.[4] Jean-Noël Luc has shown that, in the nineteenth century, silence was learned as early as primary school.[5]

In Napoleonic lycées, bells, handbells and drums signalled when to be silent and when to talk. From the eighteenth until well into the twentieth century, injunctions to be silent extended beyond the classroom itself. They marked the time for meals in the refectory and the time for bed in the dormitory. In religious establishments, the collective prayers that preceded classes, eating and sleeping were a preparation for silence. According to Michel Foucault, these disciplines, and the harsh punishment of any violations, were part of the 'technology of toughening' practised in these institutions.

It is the same in the army, where 'silence in the ranks' is still today a ritual practice. In this environment, the ability to suffer in silence is a mark of honour as well as a necessity; the French used to call their army the 'great silent one' (grande muette).

In these diverse institutions, talking too much and making too much noise, like any violation of demands for silence, are seen as serious signs of a malfunctioning of the natural order. Further, in every milieu, a series of injunctions define and chart the limits of what can and what cannot be said. Among the rituals that enjoin quiet is the 'minute's silence', the history of which, to the best of my knowledge, remains to be written. It is a transposition of a religious practice to beyond the religious sphere. In this process of desacralizing silence, we find both the same injunctions and the same breaches.

The Education and Discipline of Silence

The dictionaries list other duties of silence recorded over the centuries. What they call the 'law of silence' usually refers to the keeping of secrets. It is found, they tell us by way of example, within the secret societies that impose silence by an oath and among novice freemasons and criminals. However, injunctions of this type do not come within the scope of my study.

The disciplines of silence imposed by codes of politeness and, more generally, civility, do. These were widely diffused in the nineteenth century by means of 'etiquette manuals', the best known of which, in France, was that of the Baronne Staffe.[6] They maintained that children should be seen and not heard when in the presence of adults, especially when the latter were speaking. For centuries, servants were expected not to speak unless invited to by their master or mistress. The same applied in the countryside in the case of agricultural workers and their employers. Any breach of these codes was disruptive in a way that might prove comical, as in numerous comedies of Molière.

Over and above these everyday impositions of silence, the civilization of manners which spread from at least the Renaissance, and which has been described by Norbert Elias, included increasingly powerful injunctions of silence together with an internalization of the norms. In his fine thesis entitled 'Le silence des organes' ('The silence of the organs'), Thierry Gasnier has described the gradual spread of prohibitions on belching, farting and allowing any organic manifestation – to which should be added that of sexual pleasure – to be heard. This was taken to such extremes in the nineteenth century that the expression 'green sickness' came into use to indicate the problems caused in women by the fear of farting in public.[7] Body language now aimed at silence in attitudes and words; speaking of the internal gustatory sensations was regarded as an offence against decency. 'The bodily languages of taste', writes Marie-Luce Gélard, 'now tended towards an ideal of silence and invisibility in the process of gustation.'[8] This form of discipline could extend to the silencing of a whole range of gestures and the handling of objects. Georg Simmel has observed that, from the nineteenth century, hailing someone in a public space could be seen as an act of aggression.

In the early nineteenth century, knowing when not to talk and knowing when to remain silent, faced with the noisiness indulged in by the mass of the people, was a mark of distinction, as also was knowing how to speak softly. Not to talk was also to show that you were ready to listen; and in this century of confidences and elective affinities, the silence of he who knew how to listen was revealed as of extreme value. From the middle of the seventeenth century, knowing how to remain silent was an aspect of the good manners which, in Paris, showed you were not a provincial.

A major debate about penal theory took place in the nineteenth century. On one side were those who believed in confinement in cells, the so-called Pennsylvania system, in which isolation automatically imposed permanent silence; on the other side were the proponents of the Auburn system, in which the prisoners lived and worked in a group but were required to be silent in the collective workshops. It was believed that silence might of itself lead to soul-searching, a prerequisite for the rehabilitation of the culprit. Thus it was simultaneously punishment, deprivation of freedom of speech and precondition for future reintegration into society.

To know how to keep quiet, and to be discreet, became the cornerstone of the private sphere which developed from the end of the eighteenth century. It was based on secrets or at least on the strict limitation of their circulation. The extent of the zone of silence coincided with that of the group.

Within many communities, silence is an instrument of power. 'To refuse to hear and see the other, to prevent them from leaving a mark, is to condemn them to a form of non-being.'[9] This was particularly visible in the court society described by Saint-Simon. It is useful, in this connection, to reflect on the silences of historians and on the reasons for their terseness. It is sometimes due to a lack of evidence, sometimes to a refusal to record. Either way, it is for the historian to ask what the silence means.

The demands for silence and the disciplines of silence in the contemporary world have both altered and grown weaker, though these developments are difficult to date, even approximately. Similarly, the nature of the desire for silence has been transformed and there have been changes both in the places where it is enforced and in those where it can be enjoyed. Many of the benefits previously attributed to silence have lost their attraction, while ways of experiencing it have gradually undergone drastic change.

Since the early nineteenth century, a lowering of the threshold of tolerance of noises and racket in the West has been superimposed on these developments. The history of the disciplines of and calls for silence is, accordingly, extremely complex. In the first decades of the nineteenth century, the sound landscape in the great cities of the West, in particular Paris, by contrast with that of the countryside, was one of constant din, and there was a high threshold of tolerance of noise. Since the dawn of modern times, the street cries of craftsmen and traders had created a constant clamour. Street music, like that of the many balladeers and barrel organs, was not yet subject to any regulation. Noisy machines were everywhere, in shops and workshops. Jacques Léonard, who has studied this world of noise, has shown that there were forges operating on the ground floors of Parisian buildings. Bells – of parish churches, of convents and of schools and colleges – only added to the cacophony. Carriages made the level of street noise even more deafening.

From the middle of the century, however, the threshold of tolerance of noise decreased. A new desire for silence gradually led to the formulation of new requirements. Little by little, the street cries grew fewer, though it was not until the mid-twentieth century that they disappeared altogether. But postcards printed in the 1890s were already nostalgic in their presentation of the 'traditional crafts' which had once featured in the sound landscape. Street music, as Olivier Balaÿ has shown for Lyon, was increasingly regulated, as were noisy activities taking place inside buildings.[10] Among the social elites, noisiness was associated with a type of lower-class behaviour which was seen as uncivilized, and it became increasingly less acceptable.

Campaigners called for silence. New regulations were passed, new disciplines imposed. Silence began to be demanded in theatres and, even more, in concert halls, though it was slow to become the norm. In 1883, the photographer Nadar popularized a campaign against the noise of church bells, especially those that rang early in the morning.[11] He compared the racket they made to an uprising of pots and pans. In Switzerland, people mobilized against the barking of dogs. Here and there, as still today, people complained about the crowing of cocks disturbing the silence of early morning.

Legal records confirm a shift in sensibilities. I shall quote just two examples to demonstrate this. Under the July monarchy, some *boulangers* of Montauban, who were in the habit of singing at dead of night to keep their spirits up as they worked, were the subject of complaints by their neighbours; these were rejected because their singing was deemed necessary to the proper performance of their labours. By contrast, a postilion who sounded his horn from high on his stagecoach as he drove through the night-time streets was fined; this practice did not appear necessary to his job.

From the end of the nineteenth century, the smooth sound of tyres gradually replaced the rattling of carts and the clip clop of horses' hooves. However, that said, new sound signals, such as factory whistles and motorcar horns, introduced new and previously unknown noises. These new sounds had their defenders. At the beginning of the twentieth century, Luigi Russolo and the Italian Futurists rhapsodized over the sound of machines and motorcars, and then over the din of weapons of war. Russolo claimed that the noise of a fast car or of shell-fire surpassed that of Beethoven's Fifth Symphony.[12] By contrast, as we have seen, the new sound landscape drove some sensitive pedestrians to seek refuge in the silence of churches.

Overall, the radical transformation of the sound landscape dominated the history of silence and provoked reactions that militated in silence's favour. By the beginning of the twentieth century, according to Georg Simmel, passengers travelling in trains and trams now frequently observed each other in silence, which was a new phenomenon. Since the middle of the nineteenth century, as we have said, the flâneur and many busy pedestrians no longer liked to be greeted, and the conventions observed by the crowds at the great universal exhibitions were very different from the raucous scenarios of the gatherings of only a short time before. In Paris in the 1890s, posters began to appear on the façades of buildings; the number of kiosks increased, as did the number of sandwich men.[13] This turned the streets into spaces where people read, rendering obsolete the cries of the past whose purpose had been to make a presence known. Almost all that remained were the cries of newspaper vendors and the patter of pedlars.

The fighting of the First World War then changed the meaning, significance and qualities of silence. Industrial warfare was a sound hell, a great, haunting, unremitting cacophony, in which the noise of weapons and bugles mingled with the cries of rage and pain and the death rattle of the dying – until the great silence, the absolute silence, of 11 November 1918, which forcefully signalled that the world had entered the post-war period.

Previously, any silence had been a relief, even a pleasure, 'precondition for an improbable repose'. In the trenches, noise awakened and silence lulled. A 'paradoxical shame in silence' was sometimes felt, as if it was an anomaly. This point is made by Marco de Gastyne in his *L'Angoisse du Poilu* (*The Anguish of the Poilu*). 'Learning to decode noise and silence was a daily challenge' if you wanted to survive. During an attack, reported Henri Barbusse in *Le Feu* (*Under Gunfire*), it was possible, 'among the vast uproar of the guns', to distinguish with great clarity 'this surprising silence of the bullets around us'. On the battlefield, voices had 'a curious resonance'. In this time of war, silence was intimately linked to the reality of death and the experience of mourning, as shown, for example, by the long pauses interspersed throughout the Last Post. For decades, silence punctuated the commemorative ceremonies of 11 November.[14]

It was at this period that signs enjoining silence began to appear in the middle of towns. Most common was the one that read 'Hospital: silence'. We should also note, in this connection, a transformation taking place from the middle of the twentieth century. Previously, crying out had been generally tolerated, as the Christian value of redemptive pain was implicitly accepted. In the hospitals of today, however, a cry of pain is seen as somehow shocking, evidence of a failure on the part of the medical staff and a lack of self-control on the part of the patient.

In complete contrast, the cry of pleasure, which had still seemed unacceptable in the nineteenth century, is today an essential component of the footage of innumerable films and television programmes. The complaints on this subject recorded by the police in the nineteenth century, especially when the cries had been uttered by prostitutes, testifies to this massive change.[15]

Let us consider, exceptionally, the present day. A raised voice in a train is now seen as an irritation because travellers prefer peace and quiet. This was not so right up until the middle of the twentieth century, when conversation in compartments seemed normal, even a sign of good manners. Similarly, silence during a flight is welcome, and breaking it can be seen as discourteous. The same is true of the cinema.

Should we conclude that these demands for silence indicate a lowering of the threshold of tolerance for noise? Far from it. Those who, during the day, demand and appreciate silence on public transport are often the very same people who, the night before, in a club or at some gig, have tolerated levels of noise previously unknown in human history. It is as if silence and the well-being it procures were no more than intermittent needs, dependent on time and place.

5

Interlude:
Joseph and Nazareth,
or Absolute Silence

The silence of a man, Joseph, and that of a place, Nazareth, are closely linked; and they are absolute. The adoptive father of Jesus remains mute in the Scriptures. He is the patriarch of silence. Not one word of his is to be found in any of the Gospels. When Jesus lingered among the doctors in the Temple of Jerusalem, Mary and Joseph were alarmed by his absence. However, it is his mother, not his father, who reproaches him. In Bethlehem, Joseph says nothing. When he receives in a dream the word of the angel who tells him to leave for Egypt (Matthew 2:13), he remains totally silent, then obeys without uttering a single word. Joseph's death in Nazareth is silent. In short, he responded with silence to everything that concerned him in the gospel of Matthew. His silence is the understanding heart, absolute interiority. This man has contemplated Mary and Jesus all his life, and his silence goes beyond words.

Joseph illustrates what Bossuet, in the double panegyric he devoted to him, calls the gravity and the humility of silence. For Bossuet, Nazareth was, as much as a place, a time, the great time of silence. Nowhere else were the silent emotions felt, over time, so strongly.

It is probably Charles de Foucauld who has meditated most deeply on the silence of Nazareth. He wished to place it at the heart of his spiritual thinking. In his writings he constantly reiterated his desire to make his life a 'life of Nazareth', that is, a life of humility, poverty, work, obedience, charity, reverence and contemplation. He tried to explain, to relive it better, the silence of this obscure life. Mary and Joseph, conscious that they were blessed with a marvellous treasure, remained silent so as to possess it in the solitude and silence of a secluded life; and no one has practised silence like them.

Charles de Foucauld heard Jesus say, one day, referring to the ten-elevenths of the length of his life: 'I have instructed you continually, not by words but by my silence.'[1] He thought that it was when Jesus had still been in his mother's womb that the silence of adoration must have been at its height. Mary and Joseph believed, he said, that they would never again 'be able to enjoy Him . . . in a silence so perfect'.[2] With the approach of Christmas, Charles de Foucauld meditated on the life of Mary and Joseph, shared between 'immobile and silent adoration, caresses, and attentive, devoted and tender care'.[3] He imagined Mary and Joseph, when night fell, returning to sit by Jesus in his cradle, silent and content.

6

The Speech of Silence

Silence is often speech – quite apart from its tactical use, which I will discuss in the next chapter – but it is a speech that is in competition with that which is spoken aloud. 'Words stop silence from speaking', wrote Ionesco in his *Fragments of a Journal*; 'The spirit of things is not in words', said Antonin Artaud.[1]

'It is only when life is sluggish within us that we speak', wrote Maeterlinck, 'the true life, the only life that leaves a trace behind, is made up of silence alone'; and it is the 'sombre power' of silence that fills us with 'so deep a dread'.[2] The language of the soul is silence. This – to which I will return – poses a fundamental problem, says Charles du Bos, that of translating this language using words.

We may believe that speech '[comes] forth from the fullness of silence', and that this gives it its legitimacy, wrote Gabriel Marcel, who also emphasized the 'supratemporal quality of silence'.[3] According to Max Picard, the speech that is born of silence 'withers when it comes out of silence, out of the fullness of silence', of which it 'is only the other side . . . the resonance'. In silence, speech holds its breath and fills once more with original life; 'there is something silent in every word, as an abiding token of the origin of speech', and 'when two people are conversing with one another . . . a third is always present: silence is listening'.[4]

'Silence is speech transfigured. No word exists in itself; it exists only through its own silence. There is silence, indivisibly, within the smallest word', wrote Pierre Emanuel in *La Révolution parallèle* (*The Parallel Revolution*).[5] Silence, said Jean-Marie Le Clézio, in *L'Extase matérielle* (*The Material Ecstasy*), 'is the supreme outcome of language and consciousness'.[6] And Pascal Quignard asserted that 'language is not our native land. We come from silence, and we were corrupted when we still walked on all fours.'[7] This belief validated the attempt to rehabilitate language through silence, as advocated by Wittgenstein, after Thoreau, who believed that to recover possession of our words, hence of our lives, we must pass by way of silence.[8]

It is the silent speech of God in the Bible that is central to my discussion here. Let us listen to the testimony of those who are convinced, not that God hides and remains silent, but that he speaks above all when he says nothing. 'Lord, let us never forget that you speak also when you are silent', wrote Kierkegaard.[9] Pierre Coulange has discussed this silent speech of God in a magnificent chapter defining the notion of 'transcendent silence', 'the grandeur of God which is found not in action or in words but simply in his visit, in his flight (*vol*) if I may so express it'.[10] The supreme example is the primordial silence which preceded Creation, because 'before the fulfilment of this monumental work, *it was silence that reigned*, an awesome silence which was like a meditation on the unborn world', when the spirit flew, and darkness and silence enveloped everything.[11] The Psalms repeated this silent language of Creation, and Coulange quotes the many instances found throughout the Bible of the speech of a God who hides from view; one such comes in the New Testament, in the episode of the disciples on the road to Emmaus. In the sixteenth century, John of the Cross emphasized the presence of the silent word of God heard in the silent quietude of the dark night.

Many people have experienced silence as speech unuttered. Victor Hugo, in *Les Contemplations*, said that in Creation 'everything speaks': the air, the flower, the blade of grass . . .

De l'astre au ciron, l'immensité s'écoute . . .
Crois-tu que l'eau du fleuve et les arbres des bois
S'ils n'avaient rien à dire élèveraient la voix? . . .
Crois-tu que le tombeau, d'herbe et de nuit vêtu,
Ne soit rien qu'un silence? . . .
Non, tout est une voix et tout est un parfum
Tout dit dans l'infini quelque chose à quelqu'un. . . .[12]

Nous entendons le bruit du rayon que Dieu lance
La voix de ce que l'homme appelle le silence.[13]

[From the heavenly bodies to the smallest mite, the immensity listens . . . / Do you think that the waters of the river and the trees of the woods / If they had nothing to say, would raise their voices? . . . / Do you think that the tomb, covered with grass and with night, is only a silence? . . . / No, everything is a voice and everything is a perfume / Everything in infinity says something to someone. . . .

We hear the sound of the beam of light God throws / The voice of what humans calls silence.)

Maeterlinck constantly returns to his fascination with the speech of silence: 'but from the moment that we have something to say to each other, we are compelled to hold our peace . . . and no sooner do we speak than something warns us that the divine gates are closing. Thus it comes about that we hug silence to us, and are very misers of it.'[14] Silence speaks particularly in unhappiness; it is then that it caresses us, and 'the kisses of the silence of misfortune . . . can never be forgotten'.[15] I shall return at some length to the speech of silence in love.

The power of silent speech has often been proclaimed. Language, wrote Merleau-Ponty, 'lives only from silence; everything we cast to others has germinated in this great mute land which we never leave'.[16] And the link between speech and silence has been analysed in many different spheres, including music, oratory, writing, especially poetic, painting and the cinema.

Pascal Quignard, in 'La dernière leçon de musique de Tch'eng Lien' (*Tch'eng Lien's Last Music Lesson*), has his music master declare, at the end of the day, and after asking his pupil to listen to the slightest sounds – of the wind in the trees, of a paintbrush on silk, of a child peeing onto bricks: 'I've done too much music today. I shall bathe my ears in silence.' M. de Sainte Colombe, the musician in *Tous les matins du monde* (*All the World's Mornings*), has taken a vow of silence, 'tomb' of regrets. Like his friend, the painter Baugin, he believes that to paint is above all to be silent. Painting is produced in silence. In the inner world of music, like painting, any quest 'can succeed only in the deepest intimacy, in silence'.[17]

The *muta eloquentia* of painting has been a particular focus of interest and the subject of much research that I can only summarize here. 'Images are silent, but they speak in silence', wrote Max Picard; they 'remind man of life before the coming of language; they move him with a yearning for that life.'[18] Painting, wrote Lessing, is mute poetry. Eugène Delacroix would later observe: 'Silence is always impressive ... I confess my preference for the silent arts, those mute things which Poussin used to say that he professed. Words are tactless, they interrupt one's peace, demand attention ... painting and sculpture seem more serious: you have to seek them out'; the 'silent charm' of painting 'has the same power, and even seems to increase each time we look at the work'.[19]

Paul Claudel devoted one of his essays, *L'Oeil écoute* (*The eye listens*), to this mute eloquence. He discusses Dutch painting, in which he saw the landscapes as 'sources of silence'. 'We have there', he wrote, of a painting of Van de Velde, 'one of those paintings that one listens to more than one looks at'; and, of a painting by Vermeer, 'it is full of the silence of the here and now'. The scenes presented by Dutch painting had, he believed, an essential additional element, silence, and this 'made it possible to apprehend the soul, or at least listen to it'.[20]

Rembrandt, though he did not invent it, was well aware of the significance of the link between emptiness, pure space and the silence revealed by an object that catches the eye. Silence, in his paintings, is 'an invitation to remember'. One of the reasons for the fascination exercised in *The Night Watch* is that it is 'full of a strange mute noise'. In his *Stormy Landscape*, Rembrandt caught the moment when, before the thunder and the lightning, the storm was presaged by a 'thickening of the silence', such as we have all experienced at the end of a piece of organ music.[21]

Claudel, contemplating stained-glass windows, adjures the Christian soul, saying: 'This is your silence.'[22] In his *Conversations dans le Loir-et-Cher*, he was critical of the way pottery is crammed together in museums, when really each item demands to be surrounded by 'a certain expanse of solitude and silence'.[23]

Of all the specialists in the history of *la Grand Siècle*, that is, the French seventeenth century, it is Marc Fumaroli who has discussed in the greatest depth what he has called the 'school of silence' that is constituted by the painting of this period. 'The arts of the silent image speak', he says, at the end of his discussion of *muta eloquentia* in the art of Nicolas Poussin, here returning to Delacroix's reading of this work.[24] This is why painters wanted solitude and silence as they worked. According to Fumaroli, the Shroud of Turin is the most powerful representation of 'the sonority of words unspoken'.[25] It is a synthesis of the interior word linked to the divine word; it is the spoken word projected into the sensible world in which what is heard silently risks being devalued. According to Pascal, 'Christian speech is most vigorous and poignant and closest to its divine source' when it is 'faithful to its silence' and stays in the register of *oratio interior*. Silence, observes Fumaroli, is not a loss of speech but a retreat by speech into its own original, more resonant, space.[26] To paint the silent gestures of heroes then assumes great semantic power.

It creates a theatre for the silent speech offered for the contemplation of the viewer. Here we come back to the concentration on internal images proposed, as we have seen, in the 'spiritual exercises'.

For centuries, and especially in the nineteenth century, the pious images of the mysteries, joyous, sorrowful or glorious, which have supported recitation of the rosary, have been part of this meditative quest bound up with silence. In the seventeenth century, the silent poetry of the images and the talking painting of the discourse consciously echoed each other.[27] We need to understand that the people of this period looked at a painting differently from us. They contemplated it with fervour. They hoped for a silent colloquy that would inspire them in their pious practices. Today, we look at a painting with only aesthetic considerations in mind. It is the task of the historian to rediscover the old way of looking, and to explain it. The painting of solitary figures, in particular, created an 'effect of silence' which was a compelling invitation to meditation, and Fumaroli has listed and discussed certain paintings that are particularly charged with powerful silent messages.

Huysmans's character Durtal, who may be seen as the double of the author, thinks that the Flemish painters, preoccupied with their craft and 'hampered by earthly reminiscences . . . were and remained men'. They lacked that 'specific culture which is practised only in the silence and peace of the cloister'. Whereas Fra Angelico, by contrast, had the ability to attain 'the seraphic realm' in which he moved, he who 'never opened his eyes, closed in prayer, excepting to paint', who 'had never looked out on the world . . . had seen only within himself'.[28] This explained the power of the silence in his work.

Yves Bonnefoy has studied the *Resurrection* of Piero della Francesca with particular attention. This painting, he believes, calls for silence. It demands that you listen to it so as not to lose any of the qualities it accrued during its long gestation. He thought that this painting was different from those which, in the Quattrocento, imposed the silence of perspective, the product of 'simple relationships between proportions and forms'. By contrast, he suggested, the silence of Piero della Francesca was the silence of 'the commonplaceness of the world, loud with hustle and bustle, with the reflection of the blue sky in pools of water'.[29]

The scenes of the Annunciation have often and rightly been seen as dominated by a paradoxical silence. In spite of the words of the Archangel – but were they spoken? – and the brief reply, a deep silence echoes that of the inner soul of Mary. It will only be broken later, by the singing of the Magnificat. From a similar perspective, Marc Fumaroli has discussed with great insight the silences of Leonardo da Vinci's *Virgin of the Rocks*, for him the supreme masterpiece of Christian art. In the silence of the persons, everything is here 'foreshadowed, accomplished and contemplated at a distance': the Annunciation, the Nativity, the Baptism and the Cross.[30]

A little painting by Raphael, currently in the Louvre, has at some point been given the title *Silence of the Virgin*. It merits a discussion of the same type as that devoted by Fumaroli to the *Virgin of the Rocks*. We will return to the *Saint Joseph* of Georges de La Tour and to the silent depths of the conversation it imposes on the spectator (see illustration). This painter, wrote Fumaroli, is attuned to that French characteristic of never doing too much, the reserve that guarantees intensity and interiority', a constant feature of 'Gallican spirituality'.[31]

Paul Claudel, as we have seen, saw the painting of Rembrandt as a painting of silence. In fact, many artists since might be described as painters of silence, to the point where it becomes difficult to compile a list. I shall try, nevertheless. Vanitas paintings, as noted above, are imbued with a silence that is only deepened by the silence of the still lives they portray; painting, wrote Louis Marin, of 'the ontology of nothingness' to be found in the silence of objects. These paintings call for a mute, silent gaze. They invite viewers to pause in their daily activities, to contemplate the end of their life, to anticipate death. At the same time, they raise the spectre of their past life. Let us note, in this connection, the exceptional power of the *Memento mori* of Philippe de Champaigne, on display in the museum of Le Mans. Mary Magdalene and St Jerome have been the archetypal figures of this painting of the vanities, school of silence.

Many painters of the first half of the nineteenth century conveyed the speech of silence with particular intensity, most notably Caspar David Friedrich. He communicates, says Anouchka Vasak, 'a mute experience of the horizon'. *The Wanderer above the Sea of Fog* portrays a whole range of emotions, in the most profound of silences, and this mute speech acts on the spectator. In the words of Vasak, 'the wanderer, who represents me, also escapes me as something other . . . he shows me that I do not see everything, and that I wish to see, but that to see assumes something left in obscurity.'[32] What we perceive in Friedrich's painting

The Speech of Silence

is what we see when we contemplate a landscape in silence. Further, the people he paints communicate their wonder in a mute immobility. They convey a reverence which expresses the religious pathos of the authentic contemplation of nature. Certain pages of the journal of Caspar David Friedrich reveal the need he felt to listen to his inner voice, before exposing in his painting what he had seen in silence and obscurity.

To illustrate my argument by a range of painted silences, I have chosen a number of canvases in the musée d'Orsay, thus dating from the second half of the nineteenth century, which are familiar to everyone: the *Angelus* of Millet and the meditative silence of pious peasants; the sensual silence of Bouguereau's *The Birth of Venus*; the maternal contemplative silence of Berthe Morisot's *The Cradle*; the silence of despair and the impossibility of communication of Degas's *L'Absinthe* (see illustration); and, finally, another silence of two solitudes, *L'Homme et la femme* of Pierre Bonnard.

However, it was the symbolists who explored the speech of silence in most depth at this period, and the list of works of theirs that do so is long. Fernand Khnopff painted *Silence* explicitly: a gloved woman puts a finger to her lips (see illustration). In the paintings of these symbolists, silence was often accompanied by shrouding in a veil or in the darkness of night. It accentuated the detachment of the person who, in contemplation, seeks true reality. Take, for example, the famous painting of Arnold Böcklin (1878), entitled *Isle of the Dead*. The silence here is suffocating. The rowing boat taking people to the island is itself its prisoner. The painting symbolizes both silence and the irrevocability of death. In Gustave Moreau's *Orpheus at the Tomb of Eurydice*, silence is everywhere. 'The sacred singer is quiet for ever. The great voice of beings and things is extinguished.'[33]

Other symbolist painters made explicit reference to silence in the title of their works. We may quote, in addition to Khnopff's pastel on paper, the series by Frantisek Kupka with the title *The Voice of Silence* (1903). The French painter Maurice Dennis gave the name Silencio to his house overlooking the beach of Trestrignel at Perros-Guirec.

Critics have detected another way of evoking silence in the work of later Surrealists. Thus Magritte's *Empire of Light* is above all a painting of deep silence (see illustration). Giulia Latini Mastrangelo has discussed at some length the way silence spreads across numerous canvases of Dali and gives them poignancy. *Enigma*, dated 1982, shows an ancient statue which heralds an eternal and total silence. When Dali painted *At the Seaside* (1932), he portrayed a solitary stretch of beach dominated by silence. 'In this solitude, [Dali] has produced a painting in which the landscape, through silence, communicates with our solitude and our silence.'[34] Dali seems here to have been inspired by what was then a very recent poem by García Lorca:

> Listen, my child, to the silence.
> It's an undulating silence,
> a silence
> that brings valleys and echoes down
> and bows foreheads
> to the ground.[35]

In our own day, we have all, in the presence of many paintings by Edward Hopper, felt that this artist primarily painted silence, the silence of highways, of streets and of houses, but above all the silence existing between people. I will return to this.

The discussion above, like that of painting as a school of silence, has inevitably been very brief. Many names should be added to those I have mentioned. I should have discussed the silence of objects in the work of Chardin; I should have cited those painters who have been silent in order to hear the slightest vibrations in nature, like those of the Barbizon School, in particular Théodore Rousseau, or those who, like Van Gogh, were able to suggest the silence of empty rooms, and not forgetting those who have portrayed familiar silent situations.

For my own part, I remember an experience which shows how the silence of a place makes it easier to respond to the silence of the paintings. By some happy chance, I found myself alone for an hour in a little room in a museum at Harvard, with a well-known series by Cézanne, portraying apples. By some inexplicable negligence, I was left there, uninterrupted, in absolute solitude and silence, alone in the presence of these paintings. I had often studied them in reproduction, but I felt a silent communication was established which both modified and deepened my appreciation.

The connection between silence and writing has fascinated many authors. The vertigo of the blank page is impregnated with silence, a link between nothingness and creation. At a different level, in the book of Genesis, what precedes Creation is a silent blank page. To write is derisory, said Maurice Blanchot:

a sea wall of paper against an ocean of silence. Silence – it alone has the last word. It alone holds the fragmented sense through the words. And it is towards it, in essence, that we tend ... we aspire ... when we write. To remain silent is what we all want, without knowing it, when we write.[36]

The blank page is the creative space par excellence. This was perceived by François Mauriac, who said: 'Every great work is born of silence and returns to it ... just as the Rhône crosses Lake Geneva, so a river of silence crosses the countryside of Combray and the salon of the Guermantes, without merging into it.'[37]

There are innumerable authors whose writing is a school of silence and teaches the reader to analyse its many forms. I will quote only the fine discussion by Michael O'Dwyer of François Mauriac's *Thérèse Desqueyroux*, a veritable initiation into silence for the reader. O'Dwyer identifies no fewer than ten forms of silence linked to speech: silences that convey the annihilation of the subject or the incommunicability between human beings, the silence that delivers the subject to the 'shadows of their being', the silence that is an interior voyage, the threatening silence of the other that sends back to nothingness, the silence created in order to resist the racket of the world and, of special relevance to us, the silence of reflection and the silences which suggest the inexpressible. For Mauriac, this human drama was almost always consubstantial with silence. 'That of a living creature', he wrote, 'unfolds almost always and culminates in silence.'[38]

And, still apropos writing as a school of silence, let us go further back in time and read a few verses of Albert Samain which appear in *Au Jardin de l'infante*, and which illustrate the observation of Gaston Bachelard: 'Great waves of silence ... vibrate in poems.'[39]

The Speech of Silence

Je rêve de vers doux et d'intimes ramages,
De vers à frôler l'âme ainsi que des plumages,

De vers blonds où le sens fluide se délie
Comme sous l'eau la chevelure d'Ophélie

De vers silencieux et sans rythme et sans trame
Où la rime sans bruit glisse comme une rame.

[I dream of sweet verses and intimate songs, / Of verses that brush against the soul like feathers, / Of light verses where the fluid sense floats free / Like Ophelia's hair beneath the stream / Of silent verses without rhythm and without system / Where the rhyme slides noiselessly like an oar.]

None of the silences I have discussed in this book are present here. This poem, writes Patrick Laude, is simply a school of silence, the writing of a music of silence which guides us towards 'withdrawal into the static silence of the substance of the soul'.[40]

The cinema as a school of silence deserves a series of volumes, so labyrinthine is it. Some specific features noted by the experts suggest a few guidelines. Silence presents directors with a challenge. In effect, writes Nina Nazarova, they are required to represent what is, at first sight, unrepresentable, which belongs to the sphere of the implicit, of insinuation, of innuendo.[41] However, painters and playwrights face the same problem

The silent cinema was able to convey emotions and feelings with great intensity. This is well known and everyone remembers the silent appearances of Dracula or of Frankenstein's monster in the films of Murnau, or the expressive face of Jeanne de Dreyer as Joan of Arc, not forgetting the wonder of love in the films of Charlie Chaplin. Much has been written about the speaking body in the silent film. The cry of Fay Wray in the hand of King Kong is the most silent in the history of the cinema. It proves that silence, in the silent film, is material, a palpable fact.

Nevertheless, in these films, as has been observed, it is the bodies that speak, more than the silence; and, thanks to the make-up, the exaggerated gestures and all they take from mime, these bodies are extremely expressive. With the arrival of talkies, the bodies were to some degree detached from the speech. Nor should we forget that silent films were usually accompanied by illustrative music and subtitles. This led Paul Vecchiali to claim that the true silences were in the talkies;[42] not forgetting that film music is inextricably linked to the silence that governs it.

In fact, cinematographic writing was for a long time of extreme subtlety: the silence of talking films 'acted as a resonating chamber for everything around it, it was enriched by the fracas which preceded it, by the stridency which succeeded it and by the deeper silence that framed it'; it speaks to us, 'whether it is soothing or unbearable, dense or barren'.[43] It is for the cineaste to make us feel the silence. Alain Mons says that in Antonioni's *Blow-up* 'an imaginary sound of silence is visible'; the 'choreography of the touchings' and the tension 'between the silence and the possible cry' here feed 'the noisy silence of the visible'. To which we should add what might appear a detail: the cinema has often revealed the silence of animals, at the same time as their gaze, and shown the 'silent vitality of animal time', the silence of a cow staring at you or of a cat that seems to dream, or the intense buzzing of flies.[44]

That said, films speak increasingly less in this way.

The Speech of Silence

The cinematographic writing of silence, I repeat, was of extreme subtlety and the spectator of today has generally ceased to appreciate it.

7

The Tactics of Silence

Let us now leave the silence intended to aid meditation and inner reflection to focus on the role of silence in social relations, on its advantages and disadvantages, its relationship to the shaping of the self-image and its contribution to the search for distinction; in a word, on the tactics advised by the moralists and, more generally, by all who have reflected on the benefits and harms of silence in a non-solitary life.

The art of keeping quiet had been the subject of many works and had given rise to numerous aphorisms by the end of the sixteenth century. True, spirituality was often an element in these. The muteness of Jesus in the Gospels posits silence in society as a virtue; thus Ignatius Loyola proposed an art of saying nothing modelled on the silence of Christ. In 1862, you could still read in the *Dictionnaire de théologie morale* that silence should, above all, be regarded as a virtue: it implied speaking only to the purpose, 'little rather than much, because it is difficult to speak much without blurting things out and sinning', and 'the sin is mortal because you are unable to keep a secret and you say things prejudicial to others'.[1]

Antiquity provided examples of significant silences. Solomon, in the book of Proverbs (17:28), tells us that 'he that shutteth his lips is esteemed a man of understanding'. Ajax, in Erebus, responds with a tragic silence when Ulysses speaks of their quarrel over who should inherit the armour of Achilles, which had led to his suicide. Dido, in the same place, answers Aeneas with a silence of terrifying power. And silence had been abundantly praised by the Stoics.

Aristotle believed that silence always brought its own reward. Seneca made it a virtue of the wise. Publilius Syrus produced many maxims on the subject. According to him, 'you should remain silent, or your words should be more valuable than your silence'. Dionysius Cato said: 'There is no danger in keeping quiet, there may be in speaking.'

In the early modern period, the opinion that you risked less by saying nothing than by speaking was constantly reiterated. It derived from the model of the courtier. The conviction that speech was risky was in accord with the precepts that regulated court society. Thus, the great texts which, from the sixteenth to the eighteenth century, dealt with the art of maintaining silence illustrate the civilizing process described by Norbert Elias. They were all of a piece with the internalization of norms that characterized it.

It was the *Oráculo Manual y Arte de Prudencia* (*The Courtier's Oracle* or *The Art of Worldly Wisdom*) of Baltasar Gracián rather than the more famous *Book of the Courtier* of Baldesar Castiglione that was the matrix for the art of remaining silent. Nevertheless,

Castiglione touched on the subject here and there in his book. He advised the courtier never to talk too much. It was dangerous rashly to embark on a conversation without being asked in the presence of a great prince. The grandee might well, in such a situation, refuse to answer so as to shame the one who had spoken out of turn. He would thus show himself to be the master of silence. The courtier should always think before saying what came into his head. Those who let their 'loquacity ... go beyond bounds' become 'silly and pointless'. Before breaking a silence it was wise to pay heed to the place where you were, the occasion and the necessary modesty. During the course of the conversation, you should now and again fall silent so as to allow the other to speak and 'reflect in order to reply'.[2]

The Courtier's Oracle, by the Spanish Jesuit Baltasar Gracián, was written in 1647 and had been translated into several European languages, including English and French, by the end of the seventeenth century. Gracián reflected at greater length on the tactics of silence, which he called the 'holy of holies of worldly wisdom', that is, moderation and discretion. The wise man should know how to exercise self-control. Here, Gracián was influenced by Seneca and Tacitus as well as by the Spanish maxims then much in vogue. When you met someone you didn't know, you should first test the ground. You should never talk about yourself and you should never complain. Above all, it was unbecoming to speak because you liked the sound of your own voice.[3]

To talk, that is, to form a relationship with someone, was an art, 'a school of knowledge and good manners'; it was how a man showed his worth.[4] 'He who is quick to speak is always on the point of being conquered and convinced.' Gracián went further: 'The things you want to say ought not to be said; and the things that are good to say are not good to do.'[5] The man of discretion should keep quiet when there was danger in speaking the truth.

True, ignorance frequently took refuge in the sanctuary of silence; the 'defective' found it advantageous to keep quiet because silence 'presented him as a man of mystery'. Another good reason to avoid talking was that the heart without a secret was 'an open letter'. Gracián went so far as to say: 'You should speak as if you were dictating your last will and testament.'[6] His book was contemporary with a series of treatises on the art of saying nothing which appeared between 1630 and 1684 and were aimed at forming the *honnête homme* or 'gentleman'. Yet, writes Marc Fumaroli, his manual remained throughout Europe the undisputed classic of the best education. The wise man kept sufficiently aloof to satisfy the requirement to preserve an element of silence with regard to himself, while also avoiding the ridiculousness of pontificating. The art of saying nothing was also, says Fumaroli, a way of keeping others in suspense and of manipulating the elements of 'appetite, curiosity, and surprise'.[7] That said, the art of *prudentia* was, as a tactic, far from easy.

Many moralists of the seventeenth and eighteenth centuries followed in this tradition. At this period conversation acquired huge importance. It involved alternating contemplative silence and wide-ranging conversation, without, as Montesquieu wrote, doing much listening. La Rochefoucauld observed that 'silence is the safest option for he who mistrusts himself'. He notes that people spoke little when not driven to speak by vanity. 'It requires great skill to speak, but no less to say nothing', and he distinguished three types of silence: eloquent, mocking and respectful. At all events, it was better to listen and never to force yourself to speak. It was important for coquettes and the old, in particular, to keep quiet, given their tendency to chatter thoughtlessly.[8] According to Mme de Sablé: 'Speaking too much is such a major fault that, when it comes to conversation, while what is good is brief, it is doubly good, and you gain by brevity what if often lost by garrulity'; and, she added, 'to be able to discover the inner self of another and conceal your own is the mark of a superior mind'.[9]

M. de Moncade opined that 'if people only said useful things, there would be deep silence in the world'.[10] La Bruyère noted that those who engaged in games of chance maintained 'an absolute silence' together with a level of attention of which they would have been incapable in other circumstances.[11] Dufresny described with amusement the introduction of a newcomer to the court: 'He did nothing and said nothing. He was a wise man, they said. In fact, there was wisdom in his modesty and in his silence; because if he had done something or said something, they would have known he was only a fool.'[12]

The year 1771 saw the appearance of *L'Art de se taire*, by the Abbé Dinouart, a book destined for a large readership. In it, the author recapitulated with clarity, force and in detail all that had gone before. His main message was that 'men are never more in possession of themselves than when in silence'.[13] Given the attention it attracted, I shall look at his treatise in some detail. Dinouart distinguished eleven types of silence: prudent,

artful, complaisant, spiritual and stupid, not forgetting
the silences which were a mark of approval, of disdain,
of humour, of caprice and of political acumen. His aim
was to compose a treatise of Christian civility, which
distinguished him from his predecessors. Further, he
hoped to extend *prudentia* beyond the court to the
world of Parisian salons and men of letters, in order
to counteract the philosophical spirit, rationalism and
materialism. He repeated an old opinion, found in the
Télémaque of Fénelon, to the effect that the art of good
government entailed maintaining silence. The sovereign,
more than anyone, was never more in possession of
himself than in silence.

Commenting on Dinouart's treatise, Antoine de
Baecque adds the link that it establishes between silence
and a rhetoric of the body. To be silent, in society, went
together with measured gestures, a reserved manner,
a certain facial expression and the art of the minimal
which constituted this rhetoric. Émile Moulin, writing
in 1885, said that, in society, when a man said nothing,
his silence would have no value or expression without its natural and indispensable auxiliaries, that is,
physiognomy, attitude, bearing and gaze.[14] To return to
Dinouart, he urged that one should hold one's tongue
as a Christian, as a man of the world, as a politician
and as a strategist, which, writes Antoine de Baecque,
was effectively a return to the civility of the gentleman
as propounded in the preceding century. Some of the
abbé's aphorisms sum up his strategy: 'one should cease
to remain silent only when one has something to say
which is more valuable than silence'; 'one only ever
knows how to speak well if one has previously learned
to remain silent'; 'the wise man has an expressive

silence'.[15] By contrast, the mass of the people, 'gross and stupid', do not know how to keep quiet. This is due to their want of education, their insolence and their superstition. As for silence in literature, many authors would have done well to be inspired by it and to have published nothing.

That said, wrote Émile Moulin, it can happen in society that silence is not a tactical move but simply the consequence of a trait of character, namely, 'taciturnity'. Molière has a character say of the Diafoirus son: 'You would see him, never saying a word.' Émile Moulin offered a whole spectrum of individuals who were permanently silent. Ahasuerus, according to Racine's Esther, was mute; William of Orange was surnamed the Silent. To which should be added the timid who lacked self-confidence. This led Moulin to present a series of silences which are not quite tactics and which do not correspond to the list established by Dinouart: the silences of 'inertia', of 'sangfroid', of 'incredulity', of 'doubt', of 'irony' and of 'bearing' (adopted by those who don't understand what is going on), and not forgetting the 'silence of delicacy', silence in the presence of the old, and the silences of 'respectful reserve', of politeness, of resignation and of 'dolorous sympathy'.[16]

In the nineteenth century, Senancour's Obermann criticizes those 'conversations which multiply words and do not deal with things'.[17] The eponymous hero of Benjamin Constant's novel, *Adolphe*, living in Göttingen and desperately bored, doomed by his shyness to silence, sometimes feels the urge to talk, but is held back by his disappointment with the society in which he moves, where a contemptuous silence replaces mockery.[18]

On 23 September 1854, Eugène Delacroix expounded

at length in his *Journal* on the advantages of opting to remain silent in conversation and in 'other human relationships'. His psychological analysis added depth to the earlier precepts. Unfortunately, he wrote, 'nothing is harder than such restraint for men who are dominated by their imagination. Men with subtle minds who are quick to see every side of a question find it hard to refrain from expressing what they think.' Nevertheless, 'everything is to be gained by listening. You know what you wish to say to the other man, your mind is full of it, but you cannot know what he has to say to you ... but how is it possible to resist giving a favourable idea of one's mind to a man who seems surprised and pleased to hear what one is saying?' And, 'fools are more easily carried away by the empty pleasure of listening to their own voices ... they are less interested in informing their readers than in dazzling them with their brilliance.'[19]

Gérard Genette has studied the literary purpose of the silences of Flaubert in *Madame Bovary*. For him, the narrative seems at times to fall silent, to escape beyond the walls. Bernard Masson interprets them differently. When Bovary can visit the Bertaux freely, he observes, Flaubert describes three phases in the encounters: first they exchange news in the usual country fashion, then they fall silent, having nothing to say to each other, lastly they talk as if 'the transition from silence to speech had been difficult' in the very writing of the novel, and as if the protagonists, after a short time listening to a silence 'punctuated by a few noises which accentuated its intensity', had abruptly yielded to the 'stimulus of words'.[20]

Paul Valéry belatedly joined the list of moralists of

modern times, transposing their aphorisms into the spheres of friendship and intimacy. 'True intimacy', he wrote, 'rests on a common sense of what things are *pudenda* and *tacenda*', and 'we can be truly intimate only with people having our own standard of discretion. Other qualities – character, culture, tastes – count for little'; whereas 'our true enemies are silent'.[21]

Julien Gracq describes an ingenious tactic: an interlocutor will sometimes force a disconcerting silence into the middle of a conversation, one that is 'almost rude', which creates a void and leads to 'two wide eyes which look at you without saying anything – two eyes which have managed to create a silence around them'. This was the tactic adopted by the governor of Orsenna to impose his authority on Aldo in *The Opposing Shore*.[22]

Let us move to a different world. Peasants frequently made use of the tactics of silence, but in their own way, linked to the necessity for secrecy. In the nineteenth century, as is often said, the peasant was a man of few words. He spoke rarely, speech often seeming to him pointless, even in the act of prayer. The curé of Ars observed with surprise that a peasant of his small parish regularly entered his church to adore the holy sacrament, which he did in silence, not even moving his lips. Eventually, the curé asked him what sort of piety led him to come and kneel in silence in front of the monstrance in this way. The peasant gave, by way of reply, a minimal definition of prayer: 'I perceive him, and he perceives me.' In fact he was simply transposing into the church his usual taciturn habits. In *The Earth*, Zola gives us the père Fouan, who lives for a year in a deserted house, forever maintaining his 'tragic silence', pondering projects to enlarge his estate.[23] Silence, in the countryside, was first and foremost a tactic. It was a protection against the disclosure of family secrets, and against any attack on the patrimony of honour. It promoted group solidarity. It concealed the scale of material possessions and of schemes to add to them. It masked a possible desire for vengeance. To keep quiet was to protect yourself from the gossip of others, who never let up in their efforts to penetrate what the silence kept hidden. This was a milieu where plans, ambitious or tragic, were slow to come to fruition, which meant that it was essential not to show your hand.

Quite apart from this strategic silence, the silence of the farm was reassuring. The peasant farmer valued the image of peace and quiet it presented. Everyone could speak here, observes Yvonne Crebouw, yet they were wary of speech.[24] Distrust of anyone who asked questions was not the only reason. If you kept quiet, it was because you didn't think you could interest others or because you found it difficult (or impossible) to express yourself in French. When the interlocutor was the master or a bourgeois, the social and cultural gulf was paralysing. An ancestral fear of saying too much might be fostered by the traps laid during inquisitions, by tax officials, by the police or by the magistrates. Added to which, custom sanctioned agreements which were concluded without resort to writing or even speech. The persistence of the 'communautés taisibles' of central France, and of practices of tacit or automatic renewal, was based on silence; whether in the hiring of a labourer or servant, an unwritten contract of métayage or the renewal of a contract on the same terms. The agreement was extended or ended in silence. Silence long hung over the countryside, concluded Yvonne Crebouw, preserving customs held to be sound but slowing down change.

That said, the historian confronted with the peasant world must avoid falling into the trap of exaggerating the rarity of speech and the silence of people who hardly ever opened up outside the circles in which they ordinarily lived and expressed themselves. The silence of the peasants was a fact. If they spoke rarely it was because speech was precious, and if their speech was slow, deliberate and hence easily understood, it was because they wished to be credible. In this milieu, a long prior silence pointed up the boldness of speaking. To which we should add that the silence maintained by peasant witnesses during judicial enquiries was often a sign of an incomprehension arising from a mismatch between the law code and the many sets of norms operating throughout the country. Lastly, taciturnity as practised by peasants has something of silence about it without actually being silence. It was often based on the implicit. This does not require speech. It demands knowledge of another code than that which governs speech. It supposes other forms of connivance than those based on speaking. It is encapsulated by the old saying, 'silence is consent'. Within rural society, especially in the nineteenth century, the interaction of silence and speech was highly complex. The historian must distinguish between imposed silences, deliberate silences, implicit silences, instrumentalized silences and those that were the result of a lack of mastery of the spoken word; nor should we forget the refusal of the elites to record peasant speech, regarded as impoverished, inept, even incomprehensible.

It was on all of the above that Joris-Karl Huysmans based his detestation of the countryside. His novel *En rade* (*Becalmed*) is compelling evidence of this. The uncle and aunt with whom a couple of townspeople seek refuge are taciturn, and their silence, or at least the infrequency of their speech, conceals an insatiable appetite for gain. Their sole aim is to defraud their nephew and niece. They skilfully manipulate silence, making a pretence of observing the respect that was traditional when peasants spoke to Parisians. They were both of them adept at mingling the taciturn, the respectful and the hypocritical. The niece and the nephew are dealing with a couple bonded together by a tacit agreement, sealed over a lifetime. Huysmans wonderfully conveys the tactical importance of silence and of the tacit.

It would be possible, if interminable, to discuss the uses of silence in many other milieus. The army provides a training in silent gesture, and this is even more true of the activity of hunting. Thoreau, recounting his exploration of the forests of Maine, describes the behaviour of an Indian hunter: armed with a hatchet, he slipped through the undergrowth without making a sound; he had a peculiar tread, 'elastic, noiseless, and stealthy', and, as he advanced, he now and then pointed in silence 'to a single drop of blood on the handsome, shining leaves'.[25] The historian Sylvain Venayre has vividly conveyed the powerful emotions produced by the spells of silence which punctuated the progress of the great hunts conducted in exotic, often colonial, territories in the second half of the nineteenth century. The pursuit of a wild animal involved periods of lying in wait, usually lasting a long half hour, during which it was imperative to maintain, with pounding heart, an absolute silence.[26]

8

From the Silences of Love to the Silence of Hate

Silence is an essential component of a deep love. No one has expressed this better than Maurice Maeterlinck, and I shall quote him at some length: 'If it be granted to you to descend for one moment into your soul, into the depths where the angels dwell, it is not the words spoken by the creature you loved so dearly that you will recall, or the gestures that he made', but rather 'the silences that you have lived together'; it is the quality of these silences, he goes on, that reveal 'the quality of your love and your soul'. He speaks of an 'active silence' but also of one that is 'passive', a silence that sleeps, and is 'the shadow of sleep, of death or nonexistence'.[1]

Silence is 'harbinger of the special element of the unknown that is present in each love'. Here, every silence is different, and the whole fate of a love depends on 'the quality of this first silence' that descends upon two souls. If there is no harmony between two lovers in this first silence, 'there can be no love in their souls', for the silence 'between two souls' will never change: 'its nature can never alter and even until the death of the lovers' it will retain 'the form, the attitude and the power' it had when 'for the first time, it came into the room'.[2] Words, Maeterlinck continues, 'can never express the real, special relationship that exists between two beings'. More generally, it is only in silence that we can perceive our truth about love, death and destiny.[3] 'If I tell someone I love them – as I may have told a hundred others – my words will convey nothing to him; but the silence which will ensue, if indeed I do love him, will . . . give birth to a conviction, that shall itself be silent.'[4] In conclusion, Maeterlinck asks: 'Is it not silence that determines and fixes the savour of love? Deprived of it, love would lose its eternal essence and perfume. Who has not known those silent moments which separated the lips to reunite the souls?' We must constantly seek them, and there 'is no silence more docile than the silence of love . . . it is indeed the only one that we may claim for ourselves alone.'[5]

During a love affair, experienced in all its depth, awaited for years, we chatter of the ticking clock or the setting sun to give ourselves time 'to admire each other and embrace each other in another silence which the murmur of lips and thoughts cannot disturb'.[6] Here, Maeterlinck rediscovers Jean Paul [Johann Paul Friedrich Richter], who wrote: 'When I wish to love very tenderly someone dear to me, and pardon her everything, I need only look at her for a while in silence.'[7]

Like Maeterlinck, Georges Rodenbach subscribed to the symbolist ideal of a silent communion between beings. Thus, he wrote in one of his first poems:

J'entre dans ton amour comme dans une église
Où flotte un voile bleu de silence et d'encens.[8]

[I enter into your love as into a church / In which hovers a blue veil of silence and incense.]

Elsewhere, he evokes the lover who, lying in an unlit chamber, dreams of the mistress who has killed herself:

Douceur! Ne plus se voir distincts! N'être plus qu'un!
Silence! Deux senteurs en même parfum
Penser la même chose et ne pas se le dire.[9]

[What sweetness! No longer to see ourselves distinct! To be but one! / Silence! Two aromas with a single scent / Think the same thing and do not tell each other.]

In 1955, Max Picard said that, in love, there is more silence than speech. Lovers, he wrote, are conspirators, in a conspiracy of silence. The mistress listens to the silence more than to the words of her lover. 'Be silent', she seems to murmur, 'be silent', so I may hear you. 'It is easier to love when one is silent', because 'in the silence love can reach out into the remotest corners of space'. Silence is a sign of the closeness of a friendship, too. Picard, quoting Péguy, describes the friends who enjoy the pleasure of being silent together, side by side, mile after mile, hour after hour, walking silently along silent roads. 'Happy are two friends who love each other enough to be able to be silent together', in a silent countryside.[10]

The emphasis on the depth of silence in love has a long history – we need only think of courtly love; it requires us to step back in time, and to more banal considerations. In The Book of the Courtier (1580), Baldesar Castiglione states, if not exactly in connection with a silent love affair, that he 'who loves much speaks little'. Lorenzo the Magnificent is told that 'just as true lovers have glowing hearts, so they have cold tongues, with broken speech and sudden silence'.[11] Castiglione offers advice: to make his love known, the courtier should show it by his manner rather than by his words. More affection 'is sometimes revealed in a sigh, in reverence, in timidity, than a thousand words'. The lover should make his eyes 'faithful messengers to bear the embassies of his heart' – we should not forget that at this period the look was a 'touch'.[12] It is the eyes, 'kind and soft', that silently fire their arrows. It is they that silently seal the loving accord. 'They send out their rays straight to the eyes of the beloved at a moment when these are doing the same'; then 'the spirits meet'. It is the eyes that produce the 'sweet encounter'.[13] Two lovers convey by their eyes 'what is written in their heart'. They engage in a 'long and free love talk' which is not understood by the others present thanks to their 'discretion and precaution'. The eyes of the lovers whisper 'only those words that signified'.[14]

The presence of silence in the life of lovers is proclaimed by the novels of the classical age. In *L'Astrée*, the bed is a place of 'intimate favours obtained in secrecy and in silence'.[15] The image of the silence that leads to love at the heart of the earthly paradise described by Milton is surprising: when Adam and Eve come together in their bower, the poet tells us, 'silence was pleased'. Pascal wrote that 'in love, silence is of more avail than speech . . . there is an eloquence in silence that penetrates more deeply than language can'.[16]

The romantic age is here the link between the injunctions of the moralists and the subtlety of the symbolists. Faced with the dying Eleanor, Benjamin Constant's Adolphe, who no longer loves her, observes that she has retained her feelings for him. 'She was too weak to be able to say much', he said, 'but she looked at me in silence and at these times I had the impression she was begging me to give her life, which I could no longer do.'[17] In Constant's *Cécile*, the narrator's wife loves another man than her husband. One evening, spent by the three of them alone 'in a fairly unbroken silence', the husband observes 'the glances of the two lovers, their mutual understanding revealed in the slightest matter, their happiness at being together – although they could not say a word out of my hearing'; it 'plunged me into deep meditation', he writes.[18] Here, the silence cocoons the amorous glances and the desire of the two persons. After the husband has managed to break this mute alliance, he is moved by the tears shed by Cécile, who remains 'silent and still'.[19]

Senancour's Obermann believed that 'silence protects the dreams of love', but when the silence of love ceases, 'the void in which your life is quenched' began.[20] Alfred de Vigny often refers to the power of the silence that binds lovers together. In some famous lines, the poet proposes to his mistress that he wheel his shepherd's hut into a thick patch of heather:

Et là, parmi les fleurs, nous trouverons dans l'ombre
Pour nos cheveux unis un lit silencieux.[21]

[And there, among the flowers, we shall find in the shadow / A silent couch for our two heads.]

Eva, in reply, proclaims that she will go 'solitary and serene, in chaste silence'.[22]

Victor Hugo frequently returned to the theme of silence as one of the pleasures of love. In *Contemplations*, he writes of the lovers' silent walk:

From the Silences of Love to the Silence of Hate

Longtemps muets, nous contemplâmes
Le ciel où s'éteignait le jour.
Que se passait-il dans nos âmes?
Amour! Amour!

[Long silent, we watched / The sky from which day faded. /
What was happening in our souls? / Love! Love!]

In his *Sous les arbres* (*Beneath the trees*), he is more
specific about these rich moments of silence:

Ils marchaient . . . s'arrêtaient,
Parlaient, s'interrompaient, et, pendant les silences,
Leurs bouches se taisant, leurs âmes chuchotaient.[23]

[They walked . . . stopped, / Talked, interrupted each other,
and, during the silences, / Their lips falling quiet, their souls
whispered.]

The link between love and silence became a leitmotif
of the twentieth century. Proust's narrator in *In Search
of Lost Time* silently watches Albertine asleep, then
sleeps with her without making a sound:

Then, feeling that the tide of her sleep was full . . . I would
climb deliberately and noiselessly on to the bed, lie down
by her side, clasp her waist in one arm, and place my lips
upon her cheek and my free hand on her heart and then on
every part of her body in turn, so that it too was raised, like
the pearls, by her breathing . . . The sound of her breathing,
which had grown louder, might have given the illusion of the
panting of sexual pleasure, and when mine was at its climax,
I could kiss her without having interrupted her sleep.[24]

We might compare this feeling to the silence of the
bedroom in which love letters are written.

At this point, we may turn to silent dreams of love. Saint-Exupéry talked movingly of the young girl who created a kingdom 'out of the thoughts, the voice, the silences of a lover'.[25] In Albert Camus's *The Outsider*, it is in silence, on the beach, that the idyll between Marie and the narrator begins: 'I kissed her. From that point on, neither of us said anything.'[26] Much later, Pascal Quignard wrote: 'Only silence allows us to contemplate the other.'[27]

There is another silence of love, however, already suggested by Alfred de Vigny, that which is present during sex or, more generally, erotic sensuality, another aspect of our subject, to which I shall now turn. Orgasm itself, its anticipation, its culmination and its aftermath, often dictate a range of deep silences. This was the case, according to the great names of eighteenth-century erotic literature, during masturbation, especially female masturbation, then such a source of excitement to men.

By definition, the pursuit of pleasure in the act of masturbation takes place in a silence of a particular quality and flavour. The French physician Félix Roubaud quoted the case of a young man of lymphatic temperament who was incapable of ejaculating 'when he faced the test of coitus and who could succeed only in the silence of masturbation'. Doctor Léopold Deslandes quoted other cases, those of the masturbators who operated in total silence, in the living room, surrounded by their family. 'They made no or almost no movement', but there was, 'in the subject's posture, physiognomy and silence ... something unusual' which would not have eluded the man of medicine. 'It would have been impossible, in particular, to conceal from vigilant observers the ultimate thrill however experienced the masturbator.'[28]

From the Silences of Love to the Silence of Hate

Alfred Delvau's *Dictionnaire érotique moderne*, which dates from 1864, takes pleasure in emphasizing the ecstatic state of the female who is coming to orgasm. Here, it is not so much a question of voluntary silence as of the silence caused by what was then called 'la petite mort' (little death), which happened when the woman's eyes rolled upwards, and she displayed 'white eyes'.[29]

Barbey d'Aurevilly describes as essential the silence of sexual climax in 'The Crimson Curtain'. The heroine, Alberte, is a very silent person. Her whole attitude expressed the permanent depth of her silence. It culminated during sexual intercourse. Night after night, 'always, she lay, right against my heart, silent, barely speaking to me with her voice', relates the narrator; she never responded to him 'except by long embraces'. From her 'sad mouth' came nothing 'except kisses'. Unlike other women, having climaxed, 'she said not a word'.[30] This sphinx uttered 'at the very most a monosyllable'. This went on for six months. One night, Alberte was 'more silently amorous than ever ... I could hear her through her embraces. Suddenly, I heard no more. Her arms no longer pressed me to her heart.' He thought it was 'one of those swoons into which she often fell ... I was familiar with Alberte's voluptuous spasms.'[31] But this time she was dead, inert, cold, still joined to her lover under the blue cover, in the terrifying silence of the house.

At a later date, Georges Bernanos powerfully describes the sensuality of silence in his novel *Monsieur Ouine*, to which I have already referred. A poor, simple couple had come together: Hélène, daughter of old Devandomme, a local small farmer, had married the poacher Eugène, later accused of the killing of a young farm boy. The situation was hopeless. It was from Eugène that she had learned 'a certain proud male silence making her pity everyone else. Now, day and night, there was nothing left but that silence in which she took her rest, sinking into it like a gentle patient animal – that silence alone. Outside it, everything was pale or cowardly.'[32] It is because of this that she agrees to commit suicide with Eugène in the hut where they lived. After the shot came 'a patch of silence and of night'.[33]

Silence can be delightful evidence of the depth of love, but it can also be a symptom of its destruction. Often, wrote Marcel Proust, between Albertine and me, there was the obstacle of a silence probably made up of

> grievances which she now felt and which she kept to herself because she doubtless considered them irremediable, impossible to forget, unavowable, but which nevertheless created between us a significant verbal prudence on her part or an impassable barrier of silence.[34]

Let us return to the couple imagined by Huysmans in his novel *Becalmed*. The long stay in the gloomy house of the greedy and silent cousins gradually came between the young couple. The country has killed love by silence. Each now cherishes their own dream of a future alone, a silent dream which is a dream of the death of the partner. At night, they each pretend to sleep so as not to have to speak. They have nothing more to say to each other. The old couple who have put them up are themselves embarrassed, on the day they leave, by the muteness of Jacques and Louise.

Silence can have a more tragic effect. In Mauriac's *Thérèse Desqueyroux*, that of the couple, the result of a lack of communication, leads to a crime. The silence of

Bernard is the real reason for the tragic act of Thérèse. From the beginning, between the two spouses, it is silence that has made impossible 'the enchanted sphere of passionate love', it is what has destroyed them both. Thérèse gradually comes to feel that she will be annihilated by silence, that she will be trapped by it. The silence of her life consigned this woman to the 'darkness of her being',[35] and the silence of Bernard is the main motive for the crime.

And still on this tragic theme, Alfred de Vigny had earlier made his readers share the wait of Dolorida for her faithless companion, in his long poem of that name: 'How long the silence!' thinks the mistress who is going to kill her lover.[36]

In his novel *The Grass*, Claude Simon described the soundscape of the rape of Louise, in a bathroom, by the person described simply as 'the old man'. After a short struggle, the two bodies collapse in a crash,

> a cascade of noises echoing disproportionately in the still of the night . . . and after that the silence not flowing back but falling in a mass, suddenly something absolute, crushing (a ton of silence) and total, until (like a spring trickling, it gradually wore a passage beneath a screen of fallen rocks) the minuscule, multiple and vast crackling of the rain could be heard again.[37]

The fiction describing the destructive effect of silence within a couple reflects a social reality that is the subject of a fine study by Frédéric Chauvaud, *Histoire de la haine* (*History of Hate*). After a lifetime immersed in the judicial archives of the nineteenth century, Chauvaud has come to see silence as one of the chief elements in the destruction of couples, as it was explained to the hearing, when the hatred between them was made plain. The 'couples full of hatred' had been torn apart by 'simmering resentments'. They had mostly renounced violence, but opted instead for a protracted period of 'the sulks'. 'The heavy, almost interminable, silence', he writes, 'proved an invisible yet formidable weapon.' Not to speak to your partner is 'a way of demonstrating your hatred by shutting them out of your life'. Not without a trace of humour, he observes that, paradoxically, this hatred often became 'a sort of cement which ensured the longevity of the couple, far better than love could have done'; and all the more so in that this silence of hate was from time to time broken by social convention. Appearances must be preserved. In front of an audience, whoever it might be, the couple would exchange a few words so as to put people off the scent. Once 'away from prying ears', however, they reverted to not speaking and sank back into 'a charged silence'. Chauvaud discusses the origins of this willed silence. It was sometimes after a simple quarrel or trivial disagreement that two lovers or a married couple suddenly began to hate each other and swore to themselves, silently, that they would never utter another word to their partner. They were then caught up in 'a world of old hatreds', where each seemed to be keeping a list of minor grievances to nurture a dogged and hate-filled silence.[38]

Admirers of the work of Edward Hopper know how insistently he portrayed the silence that expresses distance between a man and a woman, when, for example, one of them gazes out of a window some way away from the other, or they each isolate themselves in a task that apparently absorbs them. Similarly, many filmgoers remember the silence that is the main theme of Pierre

Granier-Deferre's film *The Cat*. The two characters, played by Simone Signoret and Jean Gabin, illustrate how silence is the culmination of a deep-seated hatred, or at least of a profound disconnection. Their attitude demonstrates Chauvaud's argument that, paradoxically, this same silence gradually becomes a cement or at least a connivance between the two persons.

9

Postlude:
The Tragedy of Silence

'In silence', wrote Max Picard, 'there is present not only the power of healing and friendship but also the power of darkness and terror . . . which can erupt from the underground of silence . . . with the destructive and demonic power that is in silence.'[1]

The first form of anxiety attributable to silence, in the history of the West, was that caused by the silence of God, what Georges Simon called the 'immense epic of God's silence'.[2] I have already referred to two great silences: that of Creation, emphasized in 4 Ezra; and the long, solemn silence created by the angel of the Apocalypse on the opening of the seventh seal, which plunged the creatures into an anxious wait for the Word. And I also discussed the silence of God in chapter 6, devoted to silence as speech, noting that, with the exception of the episode of the baptism of Jesus, although the God of the Bible did not utter words distinctly, he sometimes made his silent presence known in the form of a cloud, a light breeze or puff of wind or a range of little signs which are speech. For the Orthodox, the silence of God, silence of transcendence, is a component of his nature, which is itself essentially unknowable. And last, in the Catholic France of the seventeenth century, Pascal based his theology on the existence of a hidden God (*Deus absconditus*). For him, the fact that God concealed himself deliberately and remained silent was just and useful to the faithful. The very obscurity of God reminded humankind that they were sinners. The transcendent Being should be unfathomable and enigmatic. For John of the Cross, the fact that God chose to be silent gave mankind the freedom to believe or not to believe. In his *Spiritual Canticle*, the question he poses – 'Where have you hidden?' – is a cry of love.

But there is another aspect to our subject: the silence of God is also perceived and experienced as a tragedy. His silent absence casts doubt on his very existence. Or it can be interpreted as indifference, something that has been a constant source of anger since the Old Testament was written. Is the silence of God in the face of all the evils of the world, the horror of some natural phenomena, the suffering and death not proof that he does not exist? Deep in the heart of even the most fervent Christian, the silence of God creates the impression that he is absent, and leads at times to a crisis of faith.

Outrage at this silence has provoked cries of revolt. These are explicit in numerous Old Testament texts, which have been carefully listed by Pierre Coulange. Job pleads for an explanation from the Almighty. We read in Psalm 22 a cry that will later be repeated by the crucified Jesus: 'My God, my God, why hast thou forsaken me? Why art thou so far from helping me, and from the words of my roaring? Oh my god, I cry in the daytime, but thou hearest not.' Similar complaints are found in Psalm 28. And already, in the book of Proverbs (1:28), it was written: 'Then shall they call upon me, but I will not answer.' The book of Lamentations is suffused with anger provoked by the absence of the voice of God, who conceals himself and who seems to ignore the suffering of his people. Isaiah complains: 'Verily thou art a God that hidest thyself' (45:15).

But the greatest outrage felt over the centuries is that provoked by the silence of God as it is emphasized by Matthew in the story of the Passion. In Gethsemane on the Mount of Olives, the silence (sleep) of the apostles echoes that of God, of which Jesus will eventually complain on the cross. It is this silence that induces mortal anguish and sorrow in Christ's soul. Coulange justly observes that the silence of God, at this point in the Passion, is the 'focal point' of all Scripture and all debate about the divine mystery.[3]

This urgent question has continued to be posed throughout history, even in the hearts of the greatest saints, as shown by the writings of Theresa of Avila and, much later, Theresa of the Infant Jesus, and then the confidences of Mother Theresa.

In the nineteenth century, it was surely Alfred de Vigny who uttered the fiercest cry of rage in response to the silence of God, without, for now, making God's mutism proof of his non-existence;

S'il est vrai qu'au jardin sacré des Écritures,
Le Fils de l'Homme ait dit ce qu'on voit rapporté;
Muet, aveugle et sourd au cri des créatures,
Si le Ciel nous laissa comme un monde avorté,
Le juste opposera le dédain à l'absence,

Et ne répondra plus que par un froid silence
Au silence éternel de la Divinité.⁴

[If it be true that in the sacred garden of the Scriptures, /
The Son of Man said what we see reported; / Mute, blind
and deaf to the cry of the creatures, / If Heaven abandons
us as an aborted world, / The just will oppose disdain to
absence, / And will no longer reply except with a cold
silence / To the eternal silence of the Divinity.]

This verse from his 'Le Mont des Oliviers', which has
the title 'Silence', is not wholly accurate because it was
on the cross that Jesus complained of his abandonment
by his Father. Notwithstanding, what is striking here is
Vigny's response to the silence of God: not violent revolt
but total disdain. In 1859, he said it again: 'Behave like
Buddha', he wrote, 'silence on he who never speaks';
and in 1862: 'Never speak and never write about God
... return silence for silence'; not forgetting a series of
verses he wrote but never used in a poem: 'Thus the
mute heaven has not wished to say anything to us', or
'Bishops, take care, or silence alone will respond to the
eternal silence of the Divinity.'⁵

The belief that the hidden God (*Deus absconditus*)
would never break his silence, and that this made disdain the only possible reply, did not mean the death
of God. Nevertheless, in his studio, before he wrote
'Le Mont des Oliviers', Vigny had imagined a sceptical
Christ who declared: 'I am the son of man and not the
son of God', and who cursed the whole message. That
said, Vigny was not Nietzsche.

Victor Hugo's feelings on this subject are more
ambiguous. He never ceased to believe and to hope that
God existed, but he emphatically denounced his silence:

L'être effrayant se tait au fond du ciel nocturne . . .
Rien ne répond dans l'éther taciturne.[6]

[The dreadful being is silent deep in the night sky . . . /
Nothing answers in the taciturn ether.]

And in the poem entitled 'Les Mages':

Devant notre race asservie
Le ciel se tait, et rien n'en sort . . .
L'Inconnu garde le silence.[7]

[Before our enslaved race / Heaven is silent, and nothing
comes from it . . . / The Unknown stays silent.

Readers of the New Testament are struck by another
mysterious silence, that of Jesus on numerous occasions.
During the episode of the woman taken in adultery,
when her stoning is imminent, Jesus says nothing
and looks the other way. This silence contrasts with
the clamour of her assailants. But it is effective: Jesus
delivers his message, which is to cause each of them to
consult his conscience and not to proceed to the expia-
tion laid down by the law. As we have said, silence,
here, is speech that encourages interiority. In fact, from
this perspective, it is the whole Gospel that take place in
a context of silence.

Nevertheless, for the Christian, I repeat, the silence of
God often means suffering, doubt and a questioning of
faith. The disdain of Vigny is far from the only response
and for many people, especially in the nineteenth century, the silence of God was proof of his non-existence.
Nerval, in his poem 'Le Christ aux Oliviers', which
appears in *Les Chimères* (*The Chimeras*), though without using the word 'silence', also refers to the prayer of

Postlude: The Tragedy of Silence

Christ that went unanswered:

> Et [Jésus] se prie à crier: 'Non, Dieu n'existe pas! . . .
> Frères, je vous trompais: Abîme! Abîme! Abîme! . . .
> Dieu n'est pas! Dieu n'est plus! . . .
> Tout est mort!

> [And [Jesus] started shouting, 'God does not exist! . . . /
> Brothers, I cheated you: Abyss! abyss! . . . / There is no
> God! No God now! . . . / All is dead!']

And Jesus finally cried:

> En cherchant l'oeil de Dieu, je n'ai vu qu'un orbite
> Vaste, noir et sans fond; d'où la nuit qui l'habite
> Rayonne sur le monde et s'épaissit toujours.[8]

> [I looked for God's eye, only saw a black / Bottomless
> socket pouring out its dark / Night on the world in ever
> thickening rays.]

Here, Jesus appears as the eternal victim, the sublime
madman.

Huysmans, in *The Cathedral*, describes the suffering
of an admirable Christian, the humble Madame Bavoil,
in the face of the silence of God. Falling into conversation with Durtal, she tells him of her anguish: God no
longer replies to her prayers. He is now silent. 'I no
longer have any converse or any visions', she says, 'I am
deaf and blind. God is silent to me.'[9] Durtal is himself
racked by suffering of the same type, which in his case
is not temporary:

> We question the everlasting silence and none answers;
> we wait and none comes. In vain do we proclaim Him as
> Illimitable, Incomprehensible, Unthinkable, and confess

that every effort of our reason is vain, we cannot cease to wonder, and still less cease to suffer![10]

In the twentieth century, with the growth of unbelief, the silence of God, and the incomprehension, doubt, suffering and anger it provokes, has become less prominent in the literature. Stéphane Michaud has searched for it in three contemporary writers: Paul Celan, Yves Bonnefoy and Michel Deguy. He concludes that the silence of God is absent from contemporary poetry, which consequently ignores or keeps silent about the painful responses I have just described. Few people now ask if the silence of a hidden God is speech. More generally, poetry displays a detachment, a suspension of the ancestral links between literature and religion. Thus, in the work of Celan, writes Michaud, 'the Silence is deafening, the Absence total', as nothing proves the existence of a God who would remain silent before the suffering of the people.[11]

We need, however, to be more nuanced. Philippe Jaccottet has pondered the significance of the disappearance of religions. 'What are we to do', he asks, 'in the face of this type of silence and of, almost, nothingness?' It is for poets, he says, to 'find the language which can express with supreme power the persistence of a possibility within the impossible'. They must 'try to invent ... the song of an absence', to be those who 'speak against the void'.[12]

Let us now turn to other facets of what makes the very presence of silence tragic and painful, without its oppressive aspect deriving from a form of religious impatience, anxiety or dread. Often, wrote Vigny, 'unhappiness speaks in silence'.[13] Huysmans emphasizes the depth of feeling inspired in him by the silence which resides in one's innermost being, which emerges in moments of introspection, when 'we peer down in appalling silence into a black void'.[14] We should reflect on this fear of the silence within which leads us, today, to flee from the absence of noise and from interiority.

Maeterlinck, with his usual acuity, highlighted a number of reasons for this fear of silence. It is because of its 'sombre power' that we feel such a 'deep dread of silence' and its dangerous effects. We can, at a pinch, bear silence in isolation, our own silence, but the silence of many, silence multiplied, and above all the silence of a crowd, is an unnatural burden, its inexplicable weight feared by even the strongest characters. This is why we spend so much of our lives seeking places where silence does not reign. As soon as two or three persons are gathered together, their first thought is of banishing 'the invisible enemy'. 'Of how many ordinary friendships', asks Maeterlinck, 'may it not be said that their only foundation is the common hatred of silence!'[15]

Many great works of literature testify to the various forms assumed by the fear of silence. I will attempt a partial list, which may seem fragmentary. If the serpent inspires such unease and has personified the spirit of evil, it is because it is an utterly silent creature, as Milton suggested. In a memorable phrase, Pascal described the terror he felt before 'the eternal silence of these infinite spaces'. Senancour drew close links between silence and boredom, anticipating a very contemporary concern. When Obermann left particular places, it was because of 'the weariness of their silence. They do not speak loud enough for me', he said. 'We have abandoned the turmoil of the town; the silence which encompasses us seems at first to impart a constancy and inflexibility to the hours which would be depressing to the man accustomed to the methods of a rapid life.'[16] In the country, the days seem longer than elsewhere. The grim silence can be frightening. Baudelaire described the unease that can be created by a persistent silence, like that which reigns in towns on Sundays, when the urban machine grinds to a halt.

From a quite different perspective, Byron and, thirty years later, Vigny praised the tragic heroism of a stoical silence. The wolf in one of the latter's poems knew how to die mutely and convey his message: 'Suffer and die in silence', like me; for 'silence alone is noble; the rest is weakness'.[17]

In the middle of the twentieth century, Saint-Exupéry made his readers feel the tragic silence of a lost aircraft. He enumerated all the emotions surrounding it, in particular the anguished silence of those waiting for the plane, distraught. He describes 'that silence that grows more painful minute by minute like a fatal illness'.[18] From the same tragic perspective, we should consider the silence of the eve of battle, and the lull before the storm of an attack.

This is what Julien Gracq described as the 'silence of catastrophe'; though we should not forget, from a very different perspective, the dread aroused on certain occasions by nocturnal silence, especially in the minds of children, before the stillness and the emptiness of night, waiting for the first light of dawn.[19]

This brings us to the unavoidable subject of the silences of the approach of death: those of the sickroom, of the death chamber and then of the tomb. Georges Rodenbach frequently returned to the affinity between silence and sickness. In a poem to which he gave the title 'Les malades aux fenêtres' (The sick at the windows), he sees these men and women as both victims and high priests of silence, better able than others to penetrate its essence.[20] In a sort of 'thaumaturgy of silence', through the intermediary of the invalid, the diversity of the noises is modified from within. The silence comes over them, it guides them towards death but, at the same time, it allows them to experience its most eminent dignity.[21]

'It is as though', wrote Max Picard, 'silence, driven away from everywhere else, has come to hide with the sick. It lives with them as if in the catacombs'; 'the illness came, followed by the silence', he continues, and 'the silence is . . . today. . . uncanny, for it . . . now . . . lives with the sick.'[22]

I will quote just two examples of the evocation of the silences of the deathbed. That of Monsieur Ouine in Bernanos's novel was extremely confused. The silence of his last moments, as we have seen, was like 'a tangle of snakes', a way of avoiding understanding, an education in nothingness. The silence of the death throes of Monsieur Ouine is also a way of teaching how to mock death, beyond which, it says, there is nothing.

In his novel *Der Tod des Virgil* (*The Death of Virgil*), Hermann Broch devotes many pages to describing the advance of silence in the mind of the dying poet, and the progress of 'silence to the interior of silence'.[23] When, in the novel's fourth part, the silence of the imminent death becomes clearer, Broch writes: 'The audible had sunk back into the un-manifested . . . a new silence set in – more than the absence of noise – a second and more intense silence on a loftier plane, shallow-waved, gentle, slab-shaped and smooth, like a reflection of the water's mirror above which it was laid.'[24] From this point, Virgil has the feeling of being sheltered in a 'silence that was immutable, and yet already ready to be absorbed by a new silence, prepared for an even greater silence'.[25] The poet then wonders, was he 'in a void, excluded from all inner and outer realms of being?'[26] Next there resonates, explodes, the Word, which dissolves and abolishes the world, soaring above the void, beyond the expressible and the inexpressible; and then, the last line of the book: 'Incomprehensible and unutterable for him: it was the Word beyond speech.'[27] This chimes with the intuition of Péguy that there can be no speech during paradisiacal eternity because speech can register only in time.

What we call the 'silence of death' – the 'miserly silence and massive night' of Mallarmé[28] – has meaning only for the living. But the period after a death involves a range of silences, now shrouding death, sustained by memory. First, wrote Maeterlinck, there is the silence of 'the chamber where someone will never speak again'.[29] I quote by way of example the 'little mortuary' in which lay the mother of the man Albert Camus called 'the outsider', and into which the inmates of the old people's home 'came gliding silently before slumping in their chairs, gloomy and silent'.[30]

Then there is the awareness of the silence of the familiar things of the deceased person, like the lute of Geneviève Roussel, dead in the full bloom of youth, which so moved the poet Malherbe in the early seventeenth century. Now hanging sadly on its hook, the instrument was gradually being covered with dust, while a spider, little by little, spun over it its 'powdery web'.[31]

However, it is probably the tomb most of all that brings out the feelings aroused by the silence of the dead, heightened by the memory of their voice. This theme is so common in literature and the plastic arts that I shall quote only one example, that of Victor Hugo, so strongly did he feel the silence associated with the death of his daughter Léopoldine, which he calls the 'vast and profound silence of death'.[32] There remained the hope expressed by the 'bouche de l'ombre' (mouth of shadows) of his poem, because everything in the universe speaks:

> Crois-tu que le tombeau, d'herbe et de nuit vêtu,
> Ne soit rien qu'un silence?[33]

[Do you believe that the tomb, covered by grass and by night, / Can be nothing but a silence?]

And, remembering his daughter: 'Oh! que de fois j'ai dit: Silence! elle a parlé.'[34] [O, how many times have I said: Silence! She has spoken.']

In *Les Rayons et les Ombres*, after the death of his brother Eugène, Hugo pondered the meaning of death, and those sounds capable of breaking the silence of the tomb:

> Tu n'entendras plus rien que l'herbe et la broussaille,
> Le pas du fossoyeur dont la terre tressaille,
> La chute du fruit mûr! Et par moments le chant dispersé
>   dans l'espace,
> Du bouvier qui descend dans la plaine, et qui passe
> Derrière le vieux mur![35]

[All you will now hear is the grass and the bushes, / The step of the gravedigger that makes the ground tremble, /

Ripe fruit falling! And now and again in the air, the song, / Of the herd who descends to the plain and who passes / Behind the old wall!]

I will end my book with greatest and most tragic silence of all, that which will reign when the Earth is dead, when its dissolution will be accomplished in silence, the day evoked by Vigny 'when everything will fall silent'. Let us read 'Solvet seclum', one of the *Poèmes barbares* of Leconte de Lisle:

Tourments, crimes, remords, sanglots désespérés,
Esprit et chair de l'homme, un jour vous vous tairez!
Tout se taira, dieux, rois, forçats et foules viles,
Le rauque grondement des bagnes et des villes,
Les bêtes des forêts, des monts et de la mer,
Ce qui vole et bondit et rampe en cet enfer,
Tout ce qui tremble et fuit, tout ce qui tue et mange,
Depuis le ver de terre écrasé dans la fange
Jusqu'a la foudre errant dans l'épaisseur des nuits!
D'un seul coup la nature interrompra ses bruits.

[Torments, crimes, remorse, hopeless tears, / Flesh and spirit of man, one day you will be silent! / All will be silent, gods, kings, criminals and vile crowds, / The raucous growling of prisons and cities, / The beasts of the forests, of the mountains and of the sea, / What flies and bounds and crawls in this hell, / Everything that trembles and flees, everything that kills and eats, / From the earthworm crushed in the dirt / To the thunder raging in the darkness of night! / Suddenly nature will interrupt her noises.]

This will happen 'when the World . . . stupid, blind, howling its last . . . against some universe immovable in its strength shall crack open its old and miserable crust'.

Then, 'its impure dross shall fertilize the furrows . . . where worlds are germinating'.[36] Leconte de Lisle knew nothing of the big bang and its noise, or the expanding and retracting universe, but he presented, perhaps better than anyone before him, the inexorable destruction of our planet and the tragic silence of its débris.

Notes

Chapter 1 Silence and the Intimacy of Places

1 Paul Valéry, *Tel quel*, in *Oeuvres* (Paris, 1960), vol. 2, pp. 656–7.

2 Max Picard, *Le Monde du silence* (Paris, 1954), p. 4; first pub. Erlenbach, Switzerland; trans. Stanley Godwin as *The World of Silence* (New York, 1952; repr. Wichita, Kansas, 2002), p. 18.

3 Jules Barbey d'Aurevilly, *Un Prêtre marié*, in *Romans* (Paris, 2013), p. 889.

4 Georges Rodenbach, *Bruges-la-Morte* (Paris, 1998), p. 193; trans. Mike Mitchell and Will Stone as *Bruges-la-Morte* (London, 2005).

5 Julien Gracq, *Le Rivage des Syrtes* (Paris, 2011); trans. Richard Howard as *The Opposing Shore* (London, 1993).

6 *The Silence of the Sea/Le Silence de la mer, A Novel of French Resistance During the Second World War by 'vercors'*, ed. James W. Brown and Lawrence D. Stokes, trans. Cyril Connolly (New York/Oxford, 1991), pp. 42, 72.

7 *The Silence of the Sea*, pp. 42, 43, 72, 73.
8 *The Silence of the Sea*, pp. 53, 82, 83.
9 *The Silence of the Sea*, pp. 60, 65, 90, 94.
10 Paul Claudel, *L'oeil écoute*, in *Oeuvres en prose* (Paris, 1965), p. 2740; trans. Elsie Pell as *The Eye Listens* (New York, 1950).
11 Michelle Perrot, *Histoire de chambres* (Paris, 2009), pp. 87ff.
12 Charles Baudelaire, *Le Spleen de Paris*, in *Oeuvres complètes* (Paris, 1954), pp. 292–3, 316; trans. Edward K. Kaplan as *The Parisian Prowler* (Athens and London, 1989), pp. 16, 17.
13 Joris-Karl Huysmans, *À rebours* (Paris, 1983), pp. 142–3.
14 Perrot, *Histoire de chambres*, pp. 87ff.
15 Walt Whitman, 'There was a Child went Forth', in *Leaves of Grass*.
16 Rainer Maria Rilke, *The Notebooks of Malte Laurids Brigge*, Penguin Classics, trans. Michael Hulse (London, 2009), para 16 of eBook.
17 Rilke, *The Notebooks of Malte Laurids Brigge*, para 23.
18 Rilke, *The Notebooks of Malte Laurids Brigge*, para 50.
19 Marcel Proust, *Swann's Way* (Harmondsworth, 1957), pp. 150, 61–2.
20 Jules Barbey d'Aurevilly, 'Le rideau cramoisi' (The crimson curtain), *Les Diaboliques*, in *Romans* (Paris, 2013), p. 939.
21 Victor Hugo, 'Regard jeté dans une mansarde', in *Les Rayons et les Ombres* (Paris, 1964), p. 259.
22 Hugo, 'Regard jeté dans une mansarde', pp. 262–3.

23 Émile Zola, *Le Rêve*, in *Les Rougon-Macquart* (Paris, 1966), vol. 4, p. 902; trans. Andrew Brown as *The Dream* (London, 2005), pp. 96–7.

24 Jules Verne, *Une Fantaisie du docteur Ox* (Paris, 2011), pp. 17–18. Trans. here adapted from *Dr. Ox's Experiment, and Other Stories* (Boston, 1875); see also, more recently, *A Fantasy of Dr. Ox*, trans. Andrew Brown, Foreword by Gilbert Adair (London, 2003).

25 George Bernanos, *Monsieur Ouine* (Paris, 2008), p. 49; trans. William S. Bush (Lincoln and London, 2000), pp. 21–2.

26 Bernanos, *Monsieur Ouine*, p. 50; p. 22 of Bush translation.

27 Bernanos, *Monsieur Ouine*, pp. 51; p. 23 of Bush translation.

28 Bernanos, *Monsieur Ouine*, p. 307; pp. 235–6 of Bush translation.

29 Bernanos, *Monsieur Ouine*, pp. 310–12, 329; pp. 239, 240, 254 of Bush translation.

30 Patrick Laude, *Rodenbach. Les Décors de silence* (Brussels, 1990), pp. 71, 79.

31 Picard, *World of Silence*, p. 78.

32 Georges Rodenbach, *Le Règne du silence* (Paris, 1891). All the quotations that precede and follow our taken from Georges Rodenbach, *Oeuvre poétique* (Paris, 2008), of which *Le Règne du silence* is vol. 1, pp. 77, 271, 183, 188–9, 191, 216.

33 Picard, *World of Silence*, p. 119.

34 Safia Benhaim, 'Acheminement vers la parole. Le cinéma de Philippe Garrel', *Vertigo. Esthétique et histoire du cinéma*: 'Le silence', 28 (summer 2006).

35 Picard, *World of Silence*, p. 110.

36 Picard, *World of Silence*, p. 168.
37 Joris-Karl Huysmans, *Les Foules de Lourdes* (Paris, 1911), p. 228; trans. W. H. Mitchell as *The Crowds of Lourdes* (London, 1925), pp. 188–9.
38 Joris-Karl Huysmans, *La Cathédrale* (Claremont Ferrand, 2009), p. 82; trans. Brendan King and Clara Bell as *The Cathedral* (Cambridge, 2011), p. 43.
39 Huysmans, *La Cathédrale*, pp. 99–100, 434; *The Cathedral*, pp. 52, 233.
40 Huysmans, *La Cathédrale*, p. 190; *The Cathedral*, p. 101.
41 Huysmans, *La Cathédrale*, p. 86; *The Cathedral*, p. 45.
42 *Obermann*, Étienne Pivert de Senancour (Paris, 2003), pp. 101–2; trans. Arthur Edward Waite (London, 1903), pp. 49–50.
43 Gracq, *Opposing Shore*, pp. 66, 27, 24–5, 201.

Chapter 2 The Silences of Nature
1 Maurice de Guérin, *Le Cahier vert*, in *Oeuvres complètes* (Paris, 2012), pp. 22, 72; quotations here from *Journal of Maurice de Guérin*: with an essay by Matthew Arnold, and a memoir by Sainte-Beuve (New York, 1867), pp. 91–2.
2 Leconte de Lisle, 'Dies Irae', in *Poèmes antiques* (Paris, 1994), p. 294.
3 Stéphane Mallarmé, 'L'Azur', in *Poésies* (Paris, 1989), p. 59.
4 Henry David Thoreau, *The Writings of Henry David Thoreau*, vol. VII: *Journal*, Vol. I (1837–46) (1906), read online, entry for 10 August 1838 [53] (eBook).

5 Thoreau, *The Writings of Henry David Thoreau*, entry for 10 August 1838 [66].
6 *The Heart of Thoreau's Journals*, ed. Odell Shepard (New York, 1961), p. 105 (entry for 21 January 1853).
7 *The Heart of Thoreau's Journals*, p. 86 (entry for 19 April 1852).
8 Henry David Thoreau, *Collected Works of Henry David Thoreau*, 'Natural history of Massachusetts' (eBook).
9 Henry David Thoreau, *Walden and Other Writings* (New York, 2000), pp. 105, 133.
10 Max Picard, *Le Monde du Silence* (Paris, 1954), pp. 106, 84, 87; trans. Stanley Godwin as *The World of Silence* (Wichita, Kansas, 2002), pp. 138, 113–14, 116.
11 Nicolas Klotz, *Vertigo. Esthétique et histoire du cinéma*: 'Le silence', 28 (summer 2006), pp. 89–91.
12 Jean Breschand, *Vertigo. Esthétique et histoire du cinéma*, pp. 91, 93.
13 Joseph Joubert, *Carnets*, 2 vols (Paris, 1994).
14 Maurice de Guérin, *Cahier vert*, p. 91; *Journal of Maurice de Guérin*, p. 109.
15 François René de Chateaubriand, *Génie du christianisme* (Paris, 1978), p. 566; quotations here and below from *Genius of Christianity; or, The spirit and Beauty of the Christian Religion*, trans and ed. Charles I. White (Philadelphia, 1875), p. 147 (read online/eBook).
16 Victor Hugo, 'Pleurs dans la nuit', in *Les Contemplations* (LGF, 2002), p. 408.
17 Walt Whitman, *Leaves of Grass* (eBook).

18 Georges Rodenbach, *Oeuvre poétique*, vol. 1 (2008), p. 93.

19 Gaston Bachelard, *La Poétique de l'espace* (Paris, 1957), p. 206; trans. Maria Jolas as *The Poetics of Space* (Boston, 1969), p. 230.

20 Marcel Proust, *Swann's Way* (Harmondsworth, 1957), p. 150.

21 Paul Valéry, *Tel quel*, in *Oeuvres* (Paris, 1960), vol. 2, p. 656.

22 Paul Valéry, *Mauvaises pensées et autres*, in *Oeuvres* (Paris, 1960), p. 860.

23 Philippe Jaccottet, *La Promenade sous les arbres* (Lausanne, 2009), pp. 120–1.

24 Jaccottet, *La Promenade sous les arbres*, pp. 59, 66.

25 François René de Chateaubriand, *Itinéraire de Paris à Jérusalem*, Guy Barthélemy, 'L'Orient par l'oreille', Colloque sur Chateaubriand, 9 December 2006, études-romantiques.ish-lyon.cnrs.fr, p. 4.

26 Chateaubriand, *Itinéraire de Paris à Jérusalem*, p. 7

27 Chateaubriand, *Itinéraire de Paris à Jérusalem*, p. 21.

28 For all these points, see Guy Barthélemy, *Fromentin et l'écriture du désert* (Paris, 1997).

29 Guy Barthélemy, 'Le Désert ou l'immatérialité de Dieu, une variation sur le motif de la "caravane humaine"', colloque international sur Lamartine, ed. Gertrude Durusoy (Izmir, 2004), pp. 112–13.

30 Barthélemy, 'Le Désert ou l'immatérialité de Dieu'.

31 Barthélemy, 'Le Désert ou l'immatérialité de Dieu'.

32 Barthélemy, *Fromentin et l'écriture du désert*, p. 61.

33 Barthélemy, *Fromentin et l'écriture du désert*, p. 62.

34 Eugène Fromentin, *Un Été dans le Sahara*, in *Oeuvres complètes* (Paris, 1984), p. 54.

35 Fromentin, *Un Été dans le Sahara*, p. 123.

36 Gustave Flaubert, *Voyage en Égypte*, ed. Pierre-Marc de Biasi (Paris, 1991), pp. 64–70.

37 Antoine de Saint-Exupéry, *Terre des hommes* (Paris, 1939), p. 83; trans. Lewis Galantière as *Wind, Sand and Stars* (New York, 1939), p. 122.

38 Antoine de Saint-Exupéry, *Courrier sud* (Paris, 1929), p. 36; trans. Curtis Cate as *Southern Mail/ Night Flight* (London, 2000).

39 Saint-Exupéry, *Courrier Sud*, p. 151.

40 Quoted by Claude Reichle, *La Decouverte des Alpes et la question du paysage* (Geneva, 2002), p. 71.

41 Étienne Pivert de Senancour, *Obermann* (Paris, 2003), pp. 274, 289; trans. Arthur Edward Waite (London, 1903), pp. 239, 254.

42 Senancour, *Obermann*, p. 349; p. 320 of Waite trans.

43 Senancour, *Obermann*, pp. 349–50; p. 320 of Waite trans.

44 Senancour, *Obermann*, pp. 378, 380; pp. 349, 353 of Waite trans.

45 Senancour, *Obermann*, pp. 410, 414; pp. 385, 388 of Waite trans.

46 Senancour, *Obermann*, pp. 163, 176, 421; pp. 114–15, 129, 402 of Waite trans.

47 Quotation from John Muir, *Célébrations de la nature* (Paris, 2011), p. 52.

48 Rodenbach, *Oeuvre poétique*, pp. 290, 113.

49 Émile Zola, *Une Page d'amour*, in *Les Rougon-Macquart* (Paris, 1966), vol. 4, p. 1084; trans. Jean Stewart as *A Love Affair* (London, 1957; repr. 1972), p. 251.

50 Plato, *Euthydemus* (Benjamin Jowitt online, Internet Classics archive).

51 Jules Michelet, *La Montagne* (Plan-de-la-Tour, 1983), p. 277; trans. as *The Mountain* (1872), pp. 84, 238–9, 118 (eBook).

52 Michelet, *La Montagne*, pp. 279, 126; *The Mountain*, pp. 289, 118.

53 François René de Chateaubriand, *Génie du christianisme* (Paris, 1978), p. 566; *Genius of Christianity*, p. 460.

54 Joseph Conrad, *The Shadow Line: A Confession* (1917), p. 149 (eBook).

55 Conrad, *The Shadow Line*, p. 160.

56 Conrad, *The Shadow Line*, pp. 177, 179.

57 Albert Camus, 'La mer au plus près, Journal de bord', in *L'Été* (Paris, 1959), p. 120; trans. as *The Sea Close By* (2013).

58 Albert Camus, 'Retour à Tipasa', in *L'Été* (Paris, 2014), pp. 162–3 (quotation in translation here from unattributed eBook).

59 Picard, *World of Silence*, p. 139.

60 François René de Chateaubriand, *Voyages*, in *Oeuvres complètes* (Paris, 1832), vol. VI, p. 60; François René de Chateaubriand, *Chateaubriand's Travels in America*, trans. Richard Switzer (Kentucky, 2014), p. 45.

61 Chateaubriand, *Voyages*, p. 61; *Chateaubriand's Travels*, p. 45.

62 Chateaubriand, *Voyages*, p. 113; *Chateaubriand's Travels*, p. 78.

63 Henry David Thoreau, 'A Winter Walk' (eBook).

64 Victor Hugo, 'À un riche', in *Les Voix intérieures* (Paris, 1964), p. 192.

65 Sully Prudhomme, 'Silence et nuit des bois', in *Les Solitudes*, quoted by Émile Moulin, *Le Silence. Étude morale et littéraire* (Montauban, 1885), p. 73.

66 Muir, *Célébrations de la nature*, p. 252.

67 Robert Walser, *The Walk*, trans. Christopher Middleton (Manchester, 1982; new edn London, 1992), p. 71.

68 Ann Radcliffe, *The Mysteries of Udolpho* (Oxford, 1970) pp. 6–7.

69 François René de Chateaubriand, *René*, in *Atala. René. Le Dernier Abencerage* (Paris, 1971), pp. 144–5.

70 Guy Thuillier, *Pour une histoire du quotidien au XIXe siècle en Nivernais* (Paris, 1977).

71 'Aux champs silencieux / à la virginité des herbes non foulées': Victor Hugo, 'À Olympio', in *Les Voix intérieures*, p. 225.

72 Victor Hugo, 'Aux arbres', in *Les Contemplations*, p. 229.

73 Jules Barbey d'Aurevilly, *L'Ensorcelée*, in *Romans* (Paris, 2013), pp. 380, 398; trans. Louise Collier Wilcox as *The Bewitched* (London, 1928).

74 Jules Barbey d'Aurevilly, *Un Prêtre marié*, in *Romans* (Paris, 2013), p. 894.

75 Georges Rodenbach, *Bruges-la-Morte* (Paris, 1998), p. 130; trans. Mike Mitchell and Will Stone as *Bruges-la-Morte* (London, 2005).

76 Georges Rodenbach, *Oeuvre poétique* (Paris), p. 222.

77 Rodenbach, *Oeuvre poétique*, p. 226.

78 Honoré de Balzac, *Béatrix*, in *La Comédie humaine* (Paris, 1976), vol. 2, pp. 640, 642, 644, 655, 659,

678; trans. Katherine Prescott Wormeley as *Beatrix*
(2004) (quotations from eBook).
79 Honoré de Balzac, *Le Curé de Tours*, in *La Comédie
humaine* (Paris, 1976), vol. 4, pp. 183, 185; trans.
Katherine Prescott Wormeley as *The Vicar of Tours*
(Project Gutenberg eBook).
80 Nicole Mozet, Introduction, in Balzac, *La Comédie
humaine*, p. 175.
81 Jules Barbey d'Aurevilly, *Le Chevalier des touches*,
in *Romans* (Paris, 2013), p. 533.
82 Julien Gracq, *Le Rivage des Syrtes* (Paris, 2011);
trans. Richard Howard as *The Opposing Shore*
(London, 1993), pp. 291–2.
83 Pierre Sansot, *Du bon usage de la lenteur*, quoted by
Antoine de Baecque, in his *Écrivains randonneurs*
(Paris, 2013), p. 786.
84 François René de Chateaubriand, *Génie du christianisme* (Paris, 1978), pp. 884, 890; *Genius of
Christianity*, pp. 469, 476.
85 Picard, *Monde du silence*, pp. 106, 84, 87; *World of
Silence*, pp. 165, 163.
86 François René de Chateaubriand, *Vie de Rancé*
(Paris, 2003). See also Alain Corbin, 'Invitation
à une histoire du silence', in *Foi, fidélité, amitié
en Europe à l'époque moderne. Mélanges
offerts à Robert Sauzet* (Paris, 1995), pp.
301–11.
87 Victor Hugo, 'À l'arc de triomphe', in *Les Voix intérieures*, p. 160.

Chapter 3   The Search for Silence
1 Balthazar Alvarez, quoted by Giulia Latini
Mastrangelo, 'Le silence, voix de l'âme', in *Le*

Silence en littérature. De Mauriac à Houellebecq (Paris, 2013), p. 119.

2 Luis de Granada, *De l'oraison et de la considération* (Paris, 1863); trans. as *On Prayer and Meditation* (1612; repr. Menston, 1971). For the history of the art of meditating, see Marc Fumaroli, *L'École du silence. Le sentiment des images au XVIIe siècle* (Paris, 1998), esp. pp. 234–7.

3 Maurice Giuliani, 'Écriture et silence. À l'origine des exercices spirituels d'Ignace de Loyola', in *Du Visible à l'invisible. Pour Max Milner* (Paris, 1988), vol. 2, p. 112.

4 Ignace de Loyola, *Exercices spirituels, précédés du Testament* (Paris, 2002), p. 54.

5 de Loyola, *Exercices spirituels*, p. 195.

6 de Loyola, *Exercices spirituels*, pp. 208, 255.

7 St Teresa of Avila, John of the Cross, *Oeuvres* (Paris, 2012), p. 773.

8 St Teresa of Avila, John of the Cross, *Oeuvres*, p. 774.

9 St Teresa of Avila, John of the Cross, *Oeuvres*, note, p. 1033.

10 Gérald Chaix, 'Réforme et contre-Réforme catholiques. Recherches sur la chartreuse de Cologne au XVIe siècle', *Analecta cartusiana*, no. 80 (Salzburg, 1981), vol. 1, p. 67.

11 Chaix, 'Réforme et contre-Réforme catholiques', pp. 410–11.

12 Jacques-Bénigne Bossuet, 'Troisième exhortation aux ursulines de Meaux', in *Oeuvres oratoires* (Paris, 1894), vol. 6, pp. 252–3.

13 Bossuet, 'Troisième exhortation aux ursulines de Meaux', p. 246.

14 Bossuet, 'Troisième exhortation aux ursulines de Meaux', p. 242.
15 Bossuet, 'Troisième exhortation aux ursulines de Meaux', p. 246.
16 Bossuet, 'Troisième exhortation aux ursulines de Meaux', p. 241.
17 Bossuet, 'Seconde exhortation aux ursulines de Meaux', in *Oeuvres oratoires*, p. 230.
18 Bossuet, 'Seconde exhortation aux ursulines de Meaux', p. 231.
19 Bossuet, 'Seconde exhortation aux ursulines de Meaux', p. 232.
20 Bossuet, 'Second panégyrique de saint Benoît', in *Oeuvres* (Paris, 1961), p. 516.
21 Bossuet, 'Premier panégyrique de saint Benoît', in *Oeuvres*, p. 298.
22 Bossuet, 'Panégyrique de saint Benoît', in *Oeuvres*, p. 270.
23 Bossuet, 'Panégyrique de saint Benoît', in *Oeuvres*, p. 271.
24 Bossuet, 'Méditation sur le silence', in *Oeuvres oratoires*, pp. 365–6.
25 Bossuet, 'Méditation sur le silence', p. 366.
26 Bossuet, 'Méditation sur le silence', p. 367.
27 Bossuet, 'Méditation sur le silence', pp. 371, 377.
28 Bossuet, 'Méditation sur le silence', p. 378.
29 Bossuet, 'Méditation sur le silence', p. 381.
30 François René de Chateaubriand, *Vie de Rancé* (Paris, 2003), p. 220.
31 For the vanity paintings, see the beautiful catalogue *Les Vanités dans la peinture au XVIIe siècle*, Caen, Musée des Beaux-Arts, 1990; for my argument here, see Alain Tapié, 'Décomposition d'une méditation

sur la vanité' and 'Petite archéologie du vain et de la destinée'; also Louis Marin, 'Les traverses de la vanité'.

32 Mireille Lamy, 'Marthe ou Marie? Les franciscains entre action et contemplation', in *Le Silence du cloître. L'exemple des saints, XIVe–XVIIe siècle* (Clermont Ferrand, 2011), p. 63.

33 Lamy, 'Marthe ou Marie?', passim.

34 *Écrits spirituels de Charles de Foucauld* (Paris, 1951), p. 120.

35 *Écrits spirituels de Charles de Foucauld*, p. 135.

36 *Écrits spirituels de Charles de Foucauld*, p. 182.

37 *Écrits spirituels de Charles de Foucauld*, p. 220; this letter published in Charles de Foucauld, *Letters from the Desert*, trans. Barbara Lucas (London, 1977), pp. 84–5.

38 *Écrits spirituels de Charles de Foucauld*, p. 235.

39 *Écrits spirituels de Charles de Foucauld*, p. 258.

40 Michel Laroche, *La Voie du silence. Dans la tradition des Pères du désert* (Paris, 2010), p. 86. This book is particularly valuable for its clear explanation of the lineaments of orthodox theology concerning silence.

41 Margaret Parry, 'Le monastère du silence ou la recherche du Verbe', in *Silence en littérature*, referring to Charles du Bos, for whom 'the language of the soul is silence', p. 49.

42 *Obermann*, Étienne Pivert de Senancour (Paris, 2003), pp. 101–2; trans. Arthur Edward Waite (London, 1903), p. 8.

43 Quoted by Jean-Pierre Reynaud, 'La rose des ténèbres. Transparence et mystère chez Maeterlinck', in *Du Visible à l'invisible*, pp. 135, 143.

44 Thierry Laurent, 'Le silence dans l'oeuvre de Patrick Modiano', in *Silence en littérature*, p. 61.

Chapter 4 The Educations and Disciplines of Silence

1 Maurice Maeterlinck, *Le Trésor des humbles* (Brussels, 1986), p. 20; trans. Alfred Suto as *The Treasure of the Humble* (London, 1897), pp. 13–14.

2 Maeterlinck, *Le Trésor des humbles*, p. 15; *The Treasure of the Humble*, pp. 3–4.

3 François René de Chateaubriand, *Génie du christianisme* (Paris, 1978), p. 912; *Genius of Christianity*, p. 497.

4 Alain, *Propos* (Paris, 1970), vol. 2 (20 November 1927), p. 716.

5 Jean-Noël Luc, 'L'invention du jeune enfant au XIXe siècle. De la salle d'asile à l'école maternelle (1826–1887)', thèse d'État, University of Paris I Panthéon–Sorbonne, 1994.

6 Baronne Staffe, *Règles du savoir-vivre dans la société moderne* (Paris, 1891).

7 Thierry Gasnier, 'Le silence des organes', mémoire de maîtrise, EHESS, 1980.

8 Marie-Luce Gélard, ed., *Corps sensibles. Usages et langages des sens* (Nancy, 2013), pp. 78–9, 87. See also Rudy Steinmetz, 'Conceptions du corps à travers l'acte alimentaire aux XVIIe et XVIIIe siècles', *Revue d'histoire moderne et contemporaine*, 35/1 (1988), pp. 3–35.

9 Alain Corbin, 'Le mot du président', *1848; révolutions et mutations au XIXe siècle*: 'Le silence au XIXe siècle' (1994), p. 16.

10 Olivier Balaÿ and Olivier Faure, *Lyon au XIXe*

siècle. L'environnement sonore de la ville (Grenoble, 1992).

11 *Le Cas des cloches. Soumis par Nadar à M. le ministre des Cultes (– puisqu'il y en a encore un . . .) et à tous les maires, conseillers municipaux, députés et même sénateurs* (Chambery, 1883).

12 Luigi Russolo, *L'Art des bruits* [1916] (Lausanne, 1975).

13 H. Hazel Hahn, *Scenes of Parisian Modernity. Culture and Consumption in the Nineteenth Century* (Basingstoke, 2010).

14 Esteban Buch, 'Silences de la Gande Guerre', in *Entendre la guerre. Sons, musiques et silences en 14–18* (Paris, 2014). This paragraph is largely based on this fine article, from which I also take the quotations.

15 Alain Corbin, *Les Filles de noce* (Paris, 1982), passim; trans. Alan Sheridan as *Women for Hire. Prostitution and Sexuality in France after 1850* (Cambridge, MA/London, 1990).

Chapter 5 Interlude: Joseph and Nazareth, or Absolute Silence

1 *Écrits spirituels de Charles de Foucauld* (Paris, 1951), p. 135.

2 Charles de Foucauld, *Nouveaux écrits spirituels* (Paris, 1950), p. 31.

3 de Foucauld, *Nouveaux écrits spirituels*, p. 49.

Chapter 6 The Speech of Silence

1 Quoted by Pascal Quignard; see Nadia Jammal, 'La quête de ce qu'on a perdu dans *La Leçon du musique* et *Tous les matins du monde* de Pascal

Quignard', in *Le Silence en littérature. De Mauriac à Houellebecq* (Paris, 2013), p. 219.

2 Maurice Maeterlinck, *Le Trésor des humbles* (Brussels, 1986), pp. 16–17; trans. Alfred Suto as *The Treasure of the Humble* (London, 1897), pp. 5, 7–8.

3 Gabriel Marcel, in Max Picard, *Le Monde du Silence* (Paris, 1954), preface, pp. xii–xiii.

4 Picard, *Le Monde du silence* (Paris, 1960), pp. 8–10, 20; trans. Stanley Godwin as *The World of Silence* (Wichita, Kansas, 2002), pp. 24–5, 27.

5 Pierre Emmanuel, *La Révolution parallèle* (Paris, 1975).

6 Jean-Marie G. Le Clézio, *L'Extase matérielle* (Paris, 1999).

7 Pascal Quignard, *Le Voeu du silence* (Paris, 2005), introduction.

8 Sandra Laugier, 'Du silence à la langue paternelle: Thoreau et la philosophie du langage', in *Henry D. Thoreau. Les Cahiers de l'Herne* (1994), pp. 153 ff. Laugier discusses, in this context, the *Tractatus logico-philosophicus* of Wittgenstein.

9 Kierkegaard, *Papiers*, quoted by Pierre Coulange, *Quand Dieu ne répond pas. Une réflexion biblique sur le silence de Dieu* (Paris, 2013), p. 207.

10 Coulange, *Quand Dieu ne répond pas*, p. 162.

11 Coulange, *Quand Dieu ne répond pas*, p. 164.

12 Victor Hugo, 'Ce que dit la bouche d'ombre', in *Les Contemplations*, pp. 507–8, 520.

13 Victor Hugo, 'Pleurs dans la nuit', in *Les Contemplations*, p. 520.

14 Maeterlinck, *Trésor des humbles*, p. 16; *Treasure of the Humble*, pp. 5–6.

15 Maeterlinck, *Trésor des humbles*, p. 18; *Treasure of the Humble*, pp. 5–6.

16 Maurice Merleau-Ponty, *Signes*, quoted by Nina Nazarova in *Silence en littérature*, Introduction p. 7.

17 Pascal Quignard, *La Leçon de musique* and *Tous les matins du monde*, quoted by Jammal, 'La quête de ce qu'on a perdu', pp. 219, 225.

18 Picard, *Monde du Silence*, p. 65; *World of Silence*, p. 91.

19 Eugène Delacroix, *Journal 1822–1863* (Paris, 1980), pp. 476–7; trans. Lucy Norton as *The Journal of Eugène Delacroix. A Selection* (London, 1951), pp. 258–9.

20 Paul Claudel, *L'Oeil écoute*, in *Oeuvres en prose* (Paris, 1965), pp. 173, 179, 189; trans. Elsie Pell as *The Eye Listens* (New York, 1950).

21 Claudel, *L'Oeil écoute*, pp. 196, 203, 253.

22 Claudel, *L'Oeil écoute*, p. 332.

23 Paul Claudel, *Conversations dans le Loir-et-Cher*, 'Aegri somnia', *Oeuvres en prose*, p. 891.

24 Marc Fumaroli, *L'École du silence. Le sentiment des images au XVIIe siècle* (Paris, 1998), p. 191.

25 The phrase is from Paul Claudel, quoted in Fumaroli, *École du silence*, p. 194.

26 Fumaroli, *École du silence*, pp. 195–6.

27 Fumaroli, *École du silence*, p. 237.

28 Joris-Karl Huysmans, *La Cathédrale* (Claremont Ferrand, 2009), pp 166–7; trans. Brendan King and Clara Bell as *The Cathedral*, p. 88.

29 Yves Bonnefoy, *L'Inachevable. Entretiens sur la poésie* (Paris, 2010), pp. 267–8, 270.

30 Fumaroli, *École du silence*, p. 359.

31 Fumaroli, *École du silence*, p. 518.

32 Anouchka Vasak, *Météorologies. Discours sur le ciel et le climat, des Lumières au romantisme* (Paris, 2007), pp. 464–5.

33 *Le Symbolisme en Europe*, catalogue of exhibition at the Grand Palais, 1976, p. 141. This catalogue, in which all the works mentioned here appear, is crucial for my argument.

34 Giulia Latini Mastrangelo, 'Le silence, voix de l'âme', in *Silence en littérature*, p. 117.

35 Federico García Lorca, 'Silence' (trans. Scott Keeney).

36 Maurice Blanchot, *L'Espace littéraire*, quoted by Georges Simon, 'La transcendance du silence chez Sylvie Germain', in *Silence en littérature*, pp. 103–4.

37 François Mauriac, quoted by Claude Hecham, 'Le silence et la littérature dans les oeuvres autobiographiques de François Mauriac', in *Silence en littérature*, p. 329.

38 Michael O'Dwyer, 'Le leitmotiv du silence dans Thérèse Desqueyroux', in *Silence en littérature*.

39 Gaston Bachelard, *La Poétique de l'espace* (Paris, 1957), p. 164; *The Poetics of space* (Boston, 1969), p. 179.

40 Quoted by Patrick Laude, *Rodenbach. Les Décors de silence* (Brussels, 1990), pp. 15 – 16.

41 Nazarova *Silence en littérature*, Introduction.

42 Paul Vecchiali, *Vertigo. Esthétique et histoire du cinéma*: 'Le silence', 28 (summer 2006), p. 94.

43 Thomas Salvador, *Vertigo. Esthétique et histoire du cinéma*, p. 83.

44 Alain Mons, 'Le bruit-silence ou la plongée paysagère', in Jean Mottet, ed., *Les Paysages du cinéma* (Champ Vallon, 1999), pp. 244, 246.

Chapter 7 The Tactics of Silence

1 Jean-Étienne Pierrot, *Dictionnaire de théologie morale*, vol. 32 (1862), article 'Silence'; Émile Moulin, *Le Silence. Étude morale et littéraire* (Montauban, 1885), pp. 59–60.

2 Baldesar Castiglione, *The Book of the Courtier*, trans. George Bull (Harmondsworth, 1976), p. 128.

3 Baltasar Gracián, *L'Homme de cour*, preceded by an essay by Marc Fumaroli (Paris, 2010), Maxim XLII, p. 326; Maxim CXVII, p. 394; Maxim CXLI, p. 417. Trans. as *The Courtier's Oracle* or *The Art of Worldly Wisdom*.

4 On this point, see the fundamental text of Marc Fumaroli, 'La conversation', in Pierre Nora (ed.), *Les Lieux de mémoire* (Paris, 1992), tome III, vol. 2, *Les France: Traditions*, pp. 679–743.

5 Baltasar Gracián, *L'Homme de cour*, Maxim XI, p. 301; Maxim CLIX, p. 432; Maxim CLXXIX, p. 447, and the presentation by Marc Fumaroli.

6 Gracián, *L'Homme de cour*, pp. 556–7.

7 Marc Fumaroli, 'Essai sur l'homme de cour', ibid., p. 225.

8 François de La Rochefoucauld, *Oeuvres complètes* (Paris, 1964), p. 413.

9 Mme de Sablé, *Maximes*, in *Moralistes du XVIIe siècle. De Pibrac à Dufresny*, preface by Jean Lafond (Paris, 1992), p. 250.

10 M. de Moncade, *Maximes et réflexions*, in *Moralistes du XVIIe siècle*, p. 940.

11 Jean de La Bruyère, *Les Caractères*, in *Moralistes du XVIIe siècle*, p. 780.

12 Charles Dufresny, *Amusements sérieux et comiques*, in *Moralistes du XVIIe siècle*, p. 1001.

13 Abbé Dinouart, *L'Art de se taire*, preface by Antoine de Baecque (Paris, 2011), p. 36. What follows owes much to this preface.

14 Moulin, *Le Silence*, p. 19.

15 Dinouart, *L'Art de se taire*, pp. 35, 68–9, 72.

16 Moulin, *Le Silence*, pp. 21–7.

17 Étienne Pivert de Senancour, *Obermann* (Paris, 2003), p. 223; trans. Arthur Edward Waite (London, 1903), p. 182.

18 Benjamin Constant, *Adolphe*, in *Oeuvres complètes* (Paris, 1957), p. 17; trans. Leonard Hancock as *Adolphe* (Harmondsworth, 1964).

19 Eugene Delacroix, *Journal 1822–1863* (Paris, 1980), pp. 476–7; trans. Lucy Norton as *The Journal of Eugène Delacroix. A Selection* (London, 1951), p. 258.

20 Bernard Masson, in his 'Flaubert, écrivain de l'impalpable', in *Du visible à l'invisible. Pour Max Milner* (Paris, 1988), vol. 2, p. 57, quotes Gérard Genette, 'Silences de Flaubert', in *Figures I* (Paris, 1966).

21 Paul Valéry, *Choses tues*, in *Oeuvres* (Paris, 1960), pp. 488, 492.

22 Julien Gracq, *Le Rivage des Syrtes*, (Paris, 2011), p. 309; trans. Richard Howard as *The Opposing Shore* (London, 1993), p. 280.

23 Émile Zola, *La Terre*, in *Les Rougon-Macquart* (Paris, 1966), vol. 4, p. 732; trans. Douglas Parmée as *The Earth* (1980), p. 415.

24 Yvonne Crebouw, 'Dans les campagnes: silence quotidien et silence coutumier', *1848; révolutions et*

mutations au XIXe siècle: 'Le silence au XIXe siècle' (1994), pp. 51–61. This article is essential for this subject.

25 Henry David Thoreau, *The Maine Woods* (eBook).

26 Sylvain Venayre, 'Les grandes chasses', in *Histoire de l'émotion* (Paris), vol. 2: *Des Lumières à la fin du XIXe siècle*, ed. Alain Corbin (Paris, 2016).

Chapter 8 From the Silences of Love to the Silence of Hate

1 Maurice Maeterlinck, 'Le silence', in *Le Trésor des humbles* (Brussels, 1986), pp. 16–17; trans. Alfred Suto as *The Treasure of the Humble* (London, 1897), p. 6.

2 Maeterlinck, *Trésor des humbles*, pp. 20–1; *Treasure of the Humble*, pp. 15–16.

3 Maeterlinck, *Trésor des humbles*, p. 21; *Treasure of the Humble*, p. 16.

4 Maeterlinck, *Trésor des humbles*, p. 22; *Treasure of the Humble*, pp. 17–19.

5 Maeterlinck, *Trésor des humbles*, p. 22; *Treasure of the Humble*, pp. 19–-20.

6 Maeterlinck, 'Emerson', *Trésor des humbles*, p. 80.

7 Jean Paul, quoted by Maeterlinck, 'La vie profonde', *Trésor des humbles*, p. 146.

8 Georges Rodenbach, *Oeuvre poétique* (Paris), p. 139.

9 Georges Rodenbach, *Oeuvre poétique* (Paris), p. 277.

10 Max Picard, *Le Monde du silence* (Paris, 1954), pp. 69, 71, 98; trans. Stanley Baldwin as *The World of Silence* (2002), pp. 95, 98.

11 Baldesar Castiglione, *The Book of the Courtier*,

trans. George Bull (Harmondsworth, 1976), p. 259.

12 Castiglione, *Book of the Courtier*, p. 268.

13 Castiglione, *Book of the Courtier*, p. 268.

14 Castiglione, *Book of the Courtier*, p. 270.

15 Quoted by Michelle Perrot, *Histoire de chambres* (Paris, 2009), p. 103.

16 Pascal, *Discours sur les passions de l'amour*, quoted by Émile Moulin, *Le Silence. Étude morale et littéraire* (Montauban, 1885), pp. 36–7.

17 Benjamin Constant, *Adolphe*, in *Oeuvres complètes* (Paris, 195), p. 76; trans. Leonard Tancock (Harmondsworth, 1964), p. 117.

18 Benjamin Constant, *Cécile*, in *Oeuvres complètes* (Paris, 1957), p. 138; trans. Norman Cameron as *Cécile* (1951), pp. 26–7.

19 Constant, *Cécile*, pp. 26–7

20 Étienne Pivert de Senancour, *Obermann* (Paris, 2003), pp. 294, 296; trans. Arthur Edward Waite (London, Philip Wellby, 1903), pp. 260, 262.

21 Alfred de Vigny, 'La Maison du berger', *Les Destinées*, in *Oeuvres complètes* (Paris, 1986), vol. 1, p. 121.

22 de Vigny, 'La Maison du berger', p. 127.

23 Victor Hugo, *Les Contemplations* (LGF, 2002), pp. 129, 139.

24 Marcel Proust, *The Captive*, vol. 5, pp. 74–5.

25 Antoine de Saint-Exupéry, *Terre des hommes* (Paris, 1939), p. 57; trans. Lewis Galantière as *Wind, Sand and Stars* (1939).

26 Albert Camus, *The Outsider*, trans. Joseph Laredo (Harmondsworth, 1983) p. 38.

27 Pascal Quignard, *Vie secrète* (Paris, 1998), p. 86.

28 Quoted by Alain Corbin, *L'Harmonie des plaisirs. Les manières de jouir du siècle des Lumières à l'avènement de la sexologie* (Paris, 2008), pp. 135, 160.

29 Alfred Delvau, *Dictionnaire érotique moderne* (Basel, 1864), p. 231.

30 Jules Barbey d'Aurevilly, 'Le rideau cramoisi', *Les Diaboliques*, in *Romans* (Paris, 2013), p. 941.

31 Barbey d'Aurevilly, 'Le rideau cramoisi', p. 944.

32 George Bernanos, *Monsieur Ouine* (Paris, 2008), p. 49; trans. William S. Bush (Lincoln and London, 2000), p. 96.

33 Bernanos, *Monsieur Ouine*, p. 212; p. 159 of Bush translation.

34 Proust, *The Captive*, p. 110.

35 Michael O'Dwyer, 'Le leitmotiv du silence dans *Thérèse Desqueyroux*' in *Silence en littérature*, pp. 20, 19.

36 Alfred de Vigny, 'Dolorida', *Poèmes antiques et modernes*, in *Oeuvres complètes* (Paris, 1986), vol. 1, p. 61.

37 Claude Simon, *L'Herbe* (Paris, 1986), pp. 169–70; trans. Richard Howard as *The Grass* (London, 1960), p. 199.

38 Frédéric Chauvaud, *Histoire de la haine. Une passion funeste, 1830–1930* (Rennes, 2014), pp. 174, 177.

Chapter 9 Postlude: The Tragedy of Silence

1 Max Picard, *Le Monde du Silence* (Paris, 1954), p. 31; trans. Stanley Godwin as *The World of Silence* (Wichita, Kansas, 2002), p. 49.

2 Georges Simon, 'La transcendance du silence

chez Sylvie Germain', in *Silence en littérature,* p. 107.

3 Pierre Coulange, *Quand Dieu ne répond pas. Une réflexion biblique sur le silence de Dieu* (Paris, 2013), p. 24.

4 Alfred de Vigny, 'Le Mont des Oliviers', *Les Destinées*, in *Oeuvres complètes* (Paris, 1986), vol. 1, p. 153.

5 See Jean-Pierre Lassalle, 'Vigny et le silence de Dieu', in *Alfred de Vigny* (Paris, 2010), p. 388.

6 Victor Hugo, 'Horror', in *Les Contemplations*, pp. 460–1.

7 Hugo, 'Horror', p. 490.

8 Gérard de Nerval, *Les Chimères. The Chimeras*. A version by Peter Jay (London, 1984), pp. 27–9.

9 Joris-Karl Huysmans, *La Cathédrale* (Claremont Ferrand, 2009), p. 320; trans. Brendan King and Clara Bell as *The Cathedral*, p. 172.

10 Huysmans, *La Cathédrale*, p. 367; *The Cathedral*, p. 197.

11 Stéphane Michaud, 'L'absence ou le silence de Dieu dans la poésie contemporaine: Celan, Bonnefoy, Deguy', *Études* (2011), p. 509.

12 Philippe Jaccottet, 'Dieu perdu dans l'herbe', *Éléments d'un songe*, in *Oeuvres* (Paris, 2014), pp. 325–7.

13 Alfred de Vigny, 'Le Malheur', *Poèmes antiques et modernes*, in *Oeuvres complètes* (Paris, 1986), vol. 1, p. 64.

14 Huysmans, *La Cathédrale*, p. 88; *The Cathedral*, p. 46.

15 Maurice Maeterlinck, 'Le silence', in *Le Trésor des humbles* (Brussels, 1986), p. 17; trans. Alfred Suto

as *The Treasure of the Humble* (London, 1897), p. 8.

16 Étienne Pivert de Senancour, *Obermann* (Paris, 2003), pp. 274, 404; trans. Arthur Edward Waite (London, 1903), pp. 239, 379.

17 Alfred de Vigny, 'La mort du loup', *Les Destinées*, p. 145.

18 Antoine de Saint-Exupéry, *Terre des hommes* (Paris, 1939), p. 33; trans. Lewis Galantière as *Wind, Sand and Stars* (1939).

19 Philippe Jaccottet, *La Promenade sous les arbres* (Lausanne, 2009), p. 121. In many of his novels, Julien Green returned to the scene of the nocturnal terror brought on by silence.

20 Georges Rodenbach, *Oeuvre poétique* (Paris, 2008).

21 Patrick Laude, *Rodenbach. Les Décors de silence* (Brussels, 1990).

22 Picard, *Monde du Silence*, pp. 170-71; *World of Silence*, pp. 216–17.

23 Hermann Broch, *Der Tod des Virgil*; trans. Jean Starr Untermeyer as *The Death of Virgil* (London, 1945, repr. 1977).

24 Broch, *Death of Virgil*, p. 441.

25 Broch, *Death of Virgil*.

26 Broch, *Death of Virgil*, p. 478.

27 Broch, *Death of Virgil*, p. 482.

28 Stéphane Mallarmé, 'Toast funèbre à Théophile Gautier', in *Poésies* (Paris, 1989), p. 82.

29 Maurice Maeterlinck, 'Les Avertis', in *Trésor des humbles*, p. 40.

30 Albert Camus, *The Outsider*, trans. Joseph Laredo (Harmondsworth, 1983), p. 11.

31 François de Malherbe, 'Larmes du sieur Malherbe', in *Oeuvres* (Paris, 1971), p. 5.

32 Victor Hugo, 'On vit, on parle ...', in *Les Contemplations*, p. 290.

33 Victor Hugo, 'Ce que dit la bouche de l'ombre', in *Les Contemplations*, p. 508.

34 Victor Hugo, 'Oh! je fus comme fou ...', in *Les Contemplations*, p. 280.

35 Victor Hugo, *Les Rayons et les Ombres* (Paris, 1964), p. 409 (poem on verso of the announcement of the death of Eugène Hugo).

36 Leconte de Lisle, 'Solvet seclum', in *Oeuvres complètes*, vol. 3, *Poèmes barbares* (Paris, 2012), p. 294.